ELIZABETH ARROYO

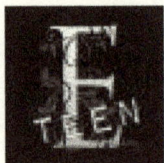

Evernight Teen ®

www.evernightteen.com

Copyright© 2025

Elizabeth Arroyo

ISBN: 978-0-3695-1270-3

Cover Artist: Jay Aheer

Editor: Stephanie Marrie

ELIZABETH ARROYO

DEDICATION

For Xe

ELIZABETH ARROYO

SOMETIMES THEY DIE

Elizabeth Arroyo

Copyright © 2025

Chapter One

Digging a grave with my hands was never easy.

Sharp rocks always found their way under my fingernails and the cold hard ground was unforgiving.

To dig the grave, I had to use what I had on hand. Right now, that was my blue ballpoint pen available in a ten pack at Wally's Mart. I was down to three. Like socks, I lost them as soon as they left my fingers. Not that I put socks on my fingers. As soon as my socks left my feet, they would grow little legs and scurry along. At least that's what Vicky always said. She did laundry and would know. Like today, I wore one green apple-colored sock and a blueberry-colored sock under my black Converse. We couldn't afford to replace my misplaced socks like we wouldn't be able to replace my pens if I continued to lose them. I still had 262 days left in the school year. I needed as many pens as I could get my hands on to finish eleventh grade.

White Falls High School was only half a mile

from my house through the woods. I'd walked this path countless times. A steady stream sat on my left, bubbling up sediment to the surface just before Mrs. Mulcahy's property. I'd found a pink feldspar on its bank once. After shaping it into a teardrop and glossing it, I had given it to my best friend Jaylene. Or rather, my ex-best friend. She broke up with me. The feldspar had matched a sweater she owned.

Thinking about Jaylene made my already gloomy day even gloomier. I didn't want to think about her. I left thoughts of Jaylene for my future self. My present self concentrated on my task at hand. Vicky always said I was too easily distracted. I had to focus on one thing at a time. And right now, it was the grave.

I used the pen to stab at the hard ground until it turned malleable and then used my fingers to dig. I didn't have a ruler, so I eyeballed the size of the hole needed to fit the remains of what I suspected to be a woodrat. Its cause of death sat haughtily beside me as if proud of the act.

"Murderer," I whispered to Mrs. Tubbs.

Her gray bushy tail swished as she continued to ignore me in favor of licking her paws. This had been Mrs. Tubbs's third catch of the week, and I suspected she left the carcass on the path so I could find it. "You are going to get me in trouble," I told the gray monstrosity. I think she was part bobcat.

The beast purred as if she didn't particularly care. I returned my attention to the woodrat. Based on its decomposition, it'd been dead for at least a few days. Rigor mortis had already set in, and the smell was the "leaving a dead fish inside a garbage can in the sun" kind of smell.

The feel of the earth between my fingers was familiar. The whole world around me stilled. My usually scattered thoughts narrowed to what my fingers were doing. For a moment, I thought of leaving the woodrat undisturbed. Let the cycle of decomposition complete itself until nothing of the carcass remained. But the thought of leaving it exposed to the elements had my skin itching. All dead things needed to be buried.

The forest trees were already starting to burst with autumn colors. A radiant orange and red. Dead leaves littered the ground. The reason I had almost missed the dead carcass near Mrs. Tubbs as I trekked to school. Had Hector not died on me, I wouldn't have been walking on this trail and would've been oblivious of the rat's rotting remains on this flat stretch of woodland.

A familiar chill lifted the hairs at the nape of my neck thinking about it just lying there. Unfound. Unburied.

Dead.

Dead things must be buried. It was the right thing to do. The moral thing to do. And Vicky always said I should live a moral life. Vicky had told me I had to think of other people's emotions since I didn't have any for myself. When God had passed out the meaning of love and empathy, he'd missed me by a day. That's what Vicky told me. Vicky tried to explain things about me without giving me real answers because she didn't *know* the real answers. She was my foster mom, not my real mom. Apparently, I had been abandoned by my real mom when she failed to pick me up from the babysitter. I was six when that happened. The county searched for my family, but they couldn't find anything, so I'd been shoved into the foster care system. At least until Vicky took me in, but she still didn't really know me.

Dirt caked the knees of my jeans. My fingers hurt. A light cool breeze carried the scent of rain which would come soon if the overhead clouds had any say in it. My hoodie did nothing to protect me against the chill of it. My body temperature always ran a touch above freezing, and my hands were always clammy. I used the back of my hand to wipe away the stray hairs on my face. I'd have to remember to ask Vicky to cut it for me. Hair growth stops at death. At least that's something to look forward to.

Though death never seems fair, everyone's ticket eventually has to be punched. That's how Mr. Harris, my boss at Harris's Funeral Home and Cremation Services, talked about dying. As if it were an awaiting adventure on a train and not a soul journey to the underground place. Everyone's ticket eventually had to be punched.

Even mine.

Mrs. Tubbs bolted seconds before I felt eyes on me, and I turned around.

My ticket would probably get punched seven minutes after Mrs. Mulcahy called the sheriff. Her still, round form stood rigid, hands on her hips. A fierce scowl pinched her features giving her a birdlike appearance. Her white hair tied up in a severe bun, her reading glasses hung over her oversized breasts by a gold chain that glinted in the sunlight. "Don't you move, you miscreant," she said, waving a finger at me. "What are you—"

That's as far as she got when her eyes found the rat beside me.

Then she fainted.

I jumped to my feet, afraid I'd just killed Mrs. Mulcahy. But nope. The woman bounced off the ground and onto her feet as if she'd hit a springboard.

"I've already called the Sheriff," she warned, her lips trembling, face pale, eyes moving from the rat back to me. She cupped the space over her heart and scurried back into her house.

The door slammed behind her as I stood rooted

like a tree. Only my roots didn't go deep because I could still lift my feet and move. I gave the rat a perusal, wondering why Mrs. Mulcahy acted as if I'd killed her cat. Woodrats were large, at least fifteen inches, and with its thick gray fur poking out of the small grave, Mrs. Mulcahy could've mistaken it for Mrs. Tubbs. I had to wonder if the cat did that on purpose. The cat hated me. Unable to find a way out of this mess, I waited for the sheriff on Mrs. Mulcahy's steps, trying to avert my eyes from the mound of dirt. The task unfinished. Thankfully, I didn't have to wait long for the sheriff.

Sheriff Johnson stood over six feet tall and had wide shoulders like a football player. It'd take two steps to move around him and another two to end up behind him. I also knew he had ripples of muscle under his shirt, and he liked showing them off by walking around shirtless at my house. A result of him and Vicky being a "thing." That's what Aimee called it. A *thing*. Sometimes he stayed over and sometimes I caught him in the living room or kitchen shirtless because of this "thing." I didn't like it, but Vicky told me I had no choice in the matter.

The *thing* remained.

Sheriff Johnson was not happy to see me. "Get in the truck."

An explanation wouldn't have made a difference, so I kept my mouth shut and planted myself in the back seat of his truck where I watched him knock on Mrs. Mulcahy's door.

I shoved my hands under my thighs to keep them warm. Despite the cooler temperatures outside marking the end of summer and beginning of autumn, Sheriff Johnson always kept the air blasting in his Bronco. It made me shiver.

Mrs. Mulcahy swung open her door and stepped onto her porch, forcing the sheriff to take a step back. She shot a glare my way, her eyes swollen from crying about Mrs. Tubbs, who wasn't even dead. I ducked behind the front seat, trying to escape the accusation in her eyes.

You killed Mrs. Tubbs.

Though I couldn't hear their exchange, it animated Sheriff Johnson. He waved his arms in the air, pointing past the tree line. Another shudder rushed through me. I may have used Mrs. Mulcahy's property as a graveyard once or twice, or fourteen times. It wasn't my fault the property had two decrepit woodsheds used by critters. And the foundation of her house was full of holes like Swiss cheese attracting all kinds of prey for her demon cat. I couldn't very well tell Mrs. Mulcahy that her cat was a killer, so she probably thought I killed them too.

Mrs. Mulcahy shook her head and then stormed inside her house and slammed the door. Sheriff Johnson looked to the sky as if it would give him answers. Seemingly getting some, or giving up, I couldn't tell, he inhaled, exhaled and started for the Bronco. He climbed in, tossed his hat on the passenger seat, and ran his hand over his buzz cut before looking at me through the rearview mirror. I should've sat on the other side to avoid his dark eyes. They made me feel uncomfortable.

"Where's your car?"

"Hector died at school yesterday."

His sigh came out long and hard. "Did you kill her cat?"

"No. That's not even her cat. It's a woodrat. Mrs. Tubbs is alive and, well, probably already setting up her next murder spree. Sir," I said. I didn't add anything else. Vicky always told me I shouldn't add more to any conversation. People would get the wrong impression of me. I had no filter. Whatever that meant.

"This is the third time she's caught you on her

property digging a grave this week." He let the statement linger. "If she catches you on her property again, she will have you arrested. Do you understand?"

"Yes, sir."

Clearly angry, he threw the truck in gear and headed into the street. He didn't say anything until we reached the front of the school two minutes later. "I'm not telling Vicky about this," he said. "She doesn't deserve this."

She didn't deserve someone like *me*. He didn't need to spell that out for me. I wanted to get out of the truck, but it only opened from the outside. I played with my fingers to keep from clawing at the door.

"Do you understand me?"

"Yes, sir," I answered.

Frustrated, he got out of the truck and opened the door for me. I sucked in a lungful of cool air.

He didn't move away from the door. "Look, I get you're a little bit odd," he said. I blinked a few times unsure where he was going with this line of questioning. He looked genuinely uncomfortable too. "Vicky told me some of it, but this thing today. If she finds out, if Mrs. Mulcahy catches you again—"

"She won't."

"Vicky will blame herself. Do you understand what I'm saying?"

Vicky had taken me in because I was a special needs case, and the state didn't know what to do with me. I learned that after hearing the whispers of everyone in town who knew and loved Vicky. She was too kind. She deserved a happy life with Sheriff Johnson. She should've returned me. Sheriff Johnson had told her the same thing too. Vicky did deserve better, but for some reason, she had chosen me, and I didn't want to mess that up.

"Yes, sir," I said. "I don't want to hurt her, sir."

"Good, but in order to do that, you have to try acting *normal*."

Like I hadn't heard that before. "I don't know how," I said honestly.

"Then fake it."

"How could I do that?"

He tapped the door frame with a knuckle. "Find someone normal and just do what they do. Act like them. When you're faced with a problem, ask yourself 'What would this *normal* person do in this situation?' See where I'm going with this?"

He wanted me to be someone else. Someone normal. Got it. "Okay. I'll try harder."

Satisfied with my answer, he smiled. Surprisingly, he had a nice smile whenever he showed it. Which actually creeped me out whenever he showed it to me. I didn't want his smile, his look, his attention. I preferred to be ignored, really.

"Give me the keys. I'll have your car fixed before you get out of school today. Good?"

I pulled out my keys from my pocket and planted them on his large open palm. "Thank you."

Seeing my dirty, scratched up hands he looked up at me. The smile a little more hesitant. "Remember," he said, "*Normal*."

I nodded.

He stepped out of my way giving me space to hop out of the truck. I pulled my backpack over my shoulder tight and didn't look back as I walked away.

Normal. Sure. I could do normal. No problem.

Chapter Two

Wrong.

Normalcy was a big fat lie. A conspiracy theory. A schema every human being sought but never attained. Because no one could define it. Normal sucked ass. Especially when every decision I'd ever made had me on the outside of the normal spectrum. Way outside. And losing my best friend solidified my place in the world.

Loser.

The putrefaction of my friendship with Jaylene Cooper began on the football field during the end of summer break.

Jaylene had looked different. She'd always guarded herself of expressions. Controlled every aspect of her life. Never reactive. Like a stone statue. She didn't let anyone see what she didn't want them to see.

Except me.

And Jaylene Cooper had almost cried once when her grandmother died. No tears fell that night. She'd withdrawn into her mental safe space, and it took me three days of ignoring her flat affect to finally bring her back around. I had played her favorite music. Had read excerpts of her favorite book and had even gone over our math homework with her all while Jaylene stared at her blank white wall.

Like me, Jaylene was different. And with her I hadn't felt so alone.

Except that day in the field. The smile she wore looked all wrong. I hadn't processed that bit of information until after. I'd been too excited that she'd returned from her summer college campus tours.

Then she slid her finger down my cheek as she

scanned all my imperfections. And there were many. The dark shaggy hair that had a mind of its own, my crooked nose from breaking it after Saoirse Tanner punched me in the face in third grade and I fell off the monkey bars. My lips were too pouty and my hazel eyes too large on my face. Her scrutiny unsettled me. After eight years, we'd never crossed the friendship line. Not even out of curiosity.

"Jordan," she had said. "I'm ready to take our relationship to the next level. I want to be your girlfriend."

Just like that. And my dumbass had responded with, "Why?"

Her brow lifted a fraction. The gears turning in her head. "Don't you want to be my boyfriend?" A hint of curiosity with a dash of confusion pinched her expression. Maybe because up until that point, I had never denied her anything.

I'd given Jaylene Cooper everything she'd ever asked of me. Thinking about our friendship, she'd led me right where she wanted me, but I couldn't give her this. The quick answer was no, I didn't want to be her boyfriend. Instead, I went with, "I don't think I'm ready." The words had left my mouth like thick syrup being squeezed out of the bottle. No way of putting that back inside.

We stood there just staring at each other without a word between us. It wasn't unnatural for us to just be silent. When Jaylene had asked how she should approach sex with Danny Scott in the ninth grade, I had let her think it through. I had wondered why she would've chosen Danny and not me. I hadn't been hurt, just curious. I had thought something was wrong with me. Duh, I suffered from entamaphobia, among other things. Of course she wanted someone else, someone normal, so what had changed?

Jaylene hadn't spoken for many minutes until she finally concluded something in her mind, nodded, and walked away. Just. Like. That.

Death had punched the ticket of our friendship. If that was a thing. We'd been friends since the third grade. We met at the clinic. While waiting to see Dr. Cooper, her mom and my psychiatrist, I had watched Jaylene silently working on a puzzle. Unlike Vicky, she didn't pluck random pieces to see if they fit. She took her time and examined each piece before attempting to fit them. I had moved next to her, and we worked on the piece in silence. I don't even think she knew I was there until her mother had called her name. She had smiled at me, and it felt like a warm kiss against my cheek.

I saw her again during my following appointment and we became friends.

She didn't like hanging out inside my house, so I'd taken her walking in the woods between my house and Mrs. Mulcahy's house. While Jaylene leaned more on the concrete form of numbers and rigid order, I preferred the chaos of life and organic chemistry. Creation and death. A cycle I needed to understand. She'd never complained about my need to bury the small animals we found dead in the woods. Silently, she let me do my thing without judgment. Just like I knew she hated the color red and always gave the campus flagpole a wide berth. Sorry American Flag. Just like I knew she had a short temper whenever things didn't go her way. It was best to stay clear of her during those moments. She had been my closest friend in White Falls.

In the small space I hid in my heart for special people, like Vicky and Mr. and Mrs. Harris, I had included her. I knew I couldn't love her like *that*. But I could protect her. I could be a good friend to her. I could be a sounding board for her. I had been. I just didn't want to touch her or kiss her. I didn't want to hold her hand or *be* with her. I didn't want to be her boyfriend.

I thought it had been a phase for her. She'd realize that she really didn't want to be my girlfriend and move on. But it'd been weeks and Jaylene hadn't called, hadn't invited me to her house where I spent most of my time listening to music or just talking about stuff. I'd even stayed over a few nights a week. Her parents had loved me because I was her only real friend. And her brother Chase tolerated me. Sometimes he'd even let me wait for her in his room and we'd pass time listening to his music or talking about the latest Marvel movies.

Not anymore.

Our friendship had taken a nosedive into a deep, dark abyss never to see the light of day.

Jaylene Cooper wore her familiar smile as she walked past my locker. The one that let me believe everything would be right in the world. Captain of the debate team, honors society, likely to get out of this shit-can town and into Harvard to become a successful attorney at some high-end firm, she competed with the sun for pushing away the darkness. Perfect blonde ringlets framed her heart shaped face. She was every guy's dream, except mine.

A leech by the name of Finn Johnson, most likely to win a full ride to Alabama U on a football scholarship, had one giant possessive arm around her shoulder. Six feet of lean muscle, tanned skin, and blue eyes made them a matching pair. The perfect duo, sure to be crowned king and queen at homecoming. Cutest couple and most likely to succeed would probably be written in their yearbook. And that Vicky's thing with Sheriff Johnson could quite possibly one day make Finn my foster brother totally sucked ass.

"To her defense," Riley said beside me. "She did ask you first and you turned her down."

I slammed my locker door shut as they passed. "Whatever," I grumbled and followed Riley to the lunchroom. We picked up our lunch trays and settled into our usual table with the geeks and freaks.

"I'm just saying," Riley continued. Once he got something in his brain, I had to survive it. "There has to be something wrong with you if you turned that down." Again, he looked at the perfect collegiate pair on their way to famous perfect status. I didn't look.

"There *is* something wrong with me, remember?" I mumbled.

Riley and I had been friends ever since we were both dropped in a vat of tar and poofed with feathers during one of the most awkward bullying sprees at White Falls. A whole week that the powers at be decided was a great idea—*not*—called Freshman Week. That had been the worst week of the lower tiers' lives. Anyway, after they locked us in a room and I lost my shit, Vicky wanted everyone involved arrested. Even the school administrators. That's how my rather rare phobia had been announced to the whole school.

My fear of closed doors.

"It's the meds," Riley said without missing a beat. "I had a cousin on psychotropic meds that lowered his libido. He was hung, like dead, hung and couldn't—" Riley stuck up his index finger. "You know what I mean?" Sometimes I wished Riley came with a Google search button because I had no clue what he was talking about. He seemed to get my confusion because he clarified it. "Erection, boner, a woody...the medication affects all that shit. Trust me."

I didn't want to trust him. I wanted him to shut up and not talk about my junk. But I lifted my eyes to the beautiful Jaylene and I got nothing. No body response. No need or want to kiss her. I got nothing. And I realized one terrible truth. I'd never had an erection. I'd never— yeah never wanked off, jerked off, or choked the...I blushed. "What happened to your cousin?"

Riley shoved a spoonful of mashed potatoes in his mouth as he shrugged. "He switched out his meds with some Pez candies. They look the same. No one found out until he wrapped his car around a tree and died." He pointed at me with his empty spoon. "But he didn't die a virgin." He gave me a wink.

Thankfully, Aimee, his girlfriend, found us at that moment. "Don't listen to a word he says, Jordan."

Riley looked offended. "Me? I didn't say anything."

She made a noise like *yeah right* and switched his salad for her milk. Something they always did without talking as if they'd arranged this ritual beforehand. A thing people with *things* did. "What'd I miss?"

Before Riley could open his mouth about my lack of wanking, I blurted, "Normal. I'm working on an experiment to be normal."

Riley smirked. "Told him to stop taking his meds. See how that goes."

Aimee looked more concerned about this advice than Riley did. She was a psychology major and wanted to be a therapist when she grew up. She loved drama. "Could be risky. You have to make your own decision about that. Do your research. Maybe talk to your foster mother about it, or your doctor. You're old enough to have patient autonomy when it comes to stuff like that."

Riley nodded as if he thought of that too. I wasn't sure if stopping my medications would make me normal. "Sheriff thinks I should find some normal guy to copy."

Riley beamed. "Me. I'd be perfect."

Aimee snorted. "There's no such thing as *normal* when it comes to boys. Trust me."

"Hey."

"But—" she said, ignoring Riley. "There are candidates. What about Liam Grant?"

She lifted her eyes behind me, and I turned to see Liam Grant walking into the lunchroom with an entourage including Chase Cooper. My heart did a little jumpstart inside my chest as I watched Chase smile.

Chase Cooper didn't fit into a mold. He wore his letterman's jacket with the school's bright blue and white colors, a black t-shirt, dirty blue jeans, and combat boots. His hair pulled into a messy bun that looked good on him. His eyes were lined with kohl making them pop, and his nails were painted black. Jock, grunge, emo, rocker, Chase wore it all. "What about Chase? I know him better than Liam."

"I don't know, man. You turned down his sister," Riley said.

"She destroyed your friendship because you said no. That's unfair," Aimee admonished.

"It *was* unfair," I echoed.

"Yeah, but everyone thought you two would be together by now. I mean, you guys are perfect for each other." Riley poked his food with his fork looking like a baby who needed a diaper change.

"And why is that?" Aimee asked, taking a defensive posture. "Tell me. Why?"

Riley turned to me for help. I couldn't answer that question, so I said nothing. "They've been friends for a long time."

"And what? Boys and girls can't stay just *friends*? Automatically, they have to be more?"

This was a trick question. Riley and I just couldn't figure it out. "No," Riley said, stretching out the O sound.

Aimee glared at him for a second then turned back to me. "On second thought. Use Chase. He's cute."

Riley sneered, "Being cute doesn't make one *normal*."

"That's the first smart thing you've said, babe," Aimee said and kissed him.

Riley practically melted. The whole conversation was forgotten, and they were back to feeding each other.

I totally did not get this dating thing. It was like baby monkeys on steroids.

Chapter Three

Whoever made up the word "normal" must've never attended high school. For the past week, I'd been making observations. A perfect example, Ashton Billings the Third who went by Ash was a senior and lead guitarist in the band with the oxymoronic name of Monkey Swine. Ash also never, ever wore his t-shirts right side out. And don't get me started with Zander, also known as Zac, drummer in the same band who had no hand-eye coordination and often gave someone a concussion during gym class whenever a ball was involved. Liam, the bassist, had a thing with pencils. He always had one in his hand drumming something and was often confused for the drummer of the same ridiculous Monkey band. And then there was Chase Cooper, who broke all the molds of what normal should be because he was perfect.

Chase and Jaylene may have shared parents, but that's all they shared. Chase had long black hair and blue-gray eyes like storm clouds while Jaylene had blonde hair and bright blue eyes. Jaylene dressed to the nines while Chase wore scuffed jeans and dirty black boots, always unlaced as if he'd never learned how to tie them. He wore eyeliner and painted his nails black. Chase had always been cold and distant whenever his family was around, but whenever we were alone, he'd be nice to me. It had always confused me. Made me wonder if I'd done something wrong. Made me scrutinize myself—my clothes, my hair, how I moved, walked. I wanted him to like *me*. Not the fake me I showed everyone else. Not the fake me I'd given Jaylene.

He was the lead vocalist and guitarist in the

Monkey Swine band. He was in soccer and basketball. He had a steady girlfriend and didn't subscribe to the jock mentality. He hung out with his bandmates who weren't athletic. They were emo-looking dudes with girlfriend groupies. Chase's groupie's name was Tabatha Brannon, or Tabby, as she liked to be called. She wore scuff jeans, black tees, and boots like him. Chase could have any girl he wanted, and chose skinny, awkward Tabatha. It could only mean that he really loved her, right?

Why did that thought turn my stomach into knots?

Maybe it was because I was watching them eat their faces off. And that was unsettling. Apparently, after maybe stalking him and his band just a little bit, I realized that sucking faces was a rite of passage. Something apparently done behind the bleachers, behind trees, dumpsters, or just behind anything, really. Away from teachers who thought sucking faces should be done in private. No one else seemed to care.

"Whatcha doin'?"

I almost popped out of my hiding spot as Aimee sat down next to me. Instead, I acted as if I were just minding my own business and not stalking Monkey Swine. Stalking would be bad. Even I knew that.

"Are you looking at who I think you're looking at?" Aimee stretched her neck to peek over the bush I'd been hiding behind. Obviously, not as clandestine as I thought.

"I don't know what you're talking about." I pulled out my sketchbook and started to draw circles. Circles were soothing. Circles were safe. Eventually, I'd get it right.

She peered into my notebook. She'd seen my drawings before. Perfect circles, like onions, cabbages, and oranges. They were round. She watched me with warm brown eyes. Pretty. She wore her brown hair in a ponytail and never held my eyes for more than a second, as if afraid I'd be able to see her soul. Not that I could see a person's soul. Looking at a person's soul was not in my skillset.

Aimee had once fitted nicely into the popular crowd before she hooked up with Riley. She fit in with every group, come to think of it, and once hung out with the bands too. She blended in and had the details on practically everyone in the school. She'd used that information for her psychology papers, letting me and Riley guess who she was writing about. We had never guessed right.

"You know she put out on the first date to keep him."

"What do you mean 'put out' to keep him?"

She shrugged. "Girls think sometimes if they give guys what they want, like," she leaned into my ear and whispered, "Sex." Then pulled back after whispering the offensive word. "The guy will stay with them forever. Or at least until the end of the school year."

"Does that really work?"

Aimee shrugged. "I don't know." She plucked my notebook out of my hands and started skimming through it, stopping after a couple of pages, her brow lifting. I knew exactly the page she landed on. Circles and onions weren't the only things I drew in my notebook. "You have Mueller's anatomy class? She said draw a diagram. This is, this is a very specific person."

I pulled my notebook back. Yeah, it was a specific boy, but she didn't know which boy and never would. "Why don't you know?" I asked, reverting back to the more important topic of girls.

"Because I haven't had sex yet. I'm saving myself."

"For Riley?"

She shrugged again. "Not sure. I told him I wasn't ready, and he seemed okay with it."

"So, you don't have to have sex with boys to keep them all year."

"I don't know. The year's not over yet, silly. And why are you interested in sex?"

Because I wanted to be normal. Apparently, being sixteen and not kissing a girl wasn't normal. Burying roadkill wasn't normal. Not having a boner wasn't normal. "I just want to be a normal boy. Boys think about sex all the time, right?"

"Yeah, I guess." She nudged my shoulder with hers. "You are not *abnormal*, Jordan. You're just different. Sometimes being different is refreshing."

"And other times?" She arched a brow. "You said sometimes being different is refreshing. *Sometimes*. So what about the other times?"

"I guess you would know the answer to that."

I lowered my eyes to the book and the boy I'd drawn perfectly. From the delicate smooth neck, the tight abs, and nether regions with the slightly darker sunspot just at the ridge of his pelvis. He never seemed to care who saw him under the shower spray in the locker room and a couple of times I'd even walked in on him in Jaylene's bathroom. He'd told me not to be dumb. We were guys and had the same thing anyway. I had been looking for Jaylene's pills and he'd used her bathroom, so he was invading, not me. And I *had* looked. So sue me. Things just stayed in my head until I *had* to get them out. And drawing him had helped, but not the way I had hoped. I didn't want to think about Chase Cooper at all.

I shut the book and got to my feet. "The other times sucks, Aimee. Being *abnormal* sucks." I lifted my backpack over one shoulder and headed back into the building.

Hector had been my sixteenth birthday present from Vicky. Jaylene and I had driven him around before she left for four weeks to check out colleges and universities during the summer. I had hoped to drive her back and forth from school this year. Didn't happen. So, seeing her leaning against my car after school, hands shoved into her pockets after ignoring me for weeks sent a thrill through me. She looked tired until she caught sight of me and straightened. A smile started to lift her lips, but then she dropped it. Probably remembering she was mad at me.

"Hi," I said, trying my best at normal. "Are you okay?"

"Just tired. Didn't realize being with Finn could be so exhausting. Do you mind giving me a ride?"

Still friends. Maybe. I couldn't tell. "Of course. We're still friends, right?"

"Right," she said dryly.

I ignored the attitude and beeped the locks open, and we both got inside. My car was on its last legs, but it sputtered to life and still got me to places. After Sheriff Johnson replaced the battery the day of the rat incident, it drove nicely. I wasn't sure how long that would last.

"Are you finally going to accept the car your dad got you?" Mr. Cooper had bought Jaylene an SUV, opting for something she'd be safe in. She had called it a tank. Preferred something smaller. It was still sitting in their garage.

"Yeah, maybe."

The rest of the drive to her house was quiet. I knew not to fill the silence. It wouldn't help my cause. They lived on the fringes of town in a neighborhood of sprawling houses and ranches. I pulled into the driveway noticing Chase's empty spot.

"Thanks," she said and handed me a twenty-dollar

bill.

"What's that for?"

"Gas."

My mood improved a little bit. "Does that mean you want me to pick you up this week?"

"No. This is a one-time deal. Finn will be driving me around until I figure out what to do with that monstrosity my dad got me. He just couldn't today."

Wow. Slap to the face as expected. "That's too much then."

She frowned and dropped the cash into the seat. "Think of it as a parting gift," she said angrily and stormed out.

I had thought the conversation we had at the football field had been our friendship breakup. That the ride had been a restart to a new truce where we could still be friends. Wrong. The twenty-dollar bill had been our breakup. Like payment for being friends. It felt as if she had ripped my heart out and thrown it back at me in the guise of that twenty-dollar bill. It made me realize that people weren't always what they seemed. I hadn't only given Jaylene what I could of my heart, but I'd given her my fears, my loves, my hates. I'd given her every part of myself I could give. She knew me better than Vicky. Better than Riley. I had trusted our friendship.

And all it'd been worth was twenty bucks.

Chapter Four

I'd been an idiot when it came to Jaylene Cooper. I just wanted a friend. As pathetic as that sounded. I wanted to know that I hadn't been the only one out there like me. I liked that she and I connected on a level no one could understand. Even Vicky didn't understand our friendship. Why would someone talented, pretty, popular, rich want to hang out with someone like me? Because she was a mental mess just like me, but hid it better.

While everyone knew about my freak-out with doors, no one knew about her freak-outs at all. She'd wrapped those moments in the privacy of that house with me or with her family. We knew each other like no one else did. So why had she gone off script and wanted more?

I grunted and squeezed the steering wheel trying to hold back the anger rising from somewhere deep inside of me. A monolithic darkness that wanted to scream and rage. I wanted to scream like a real lunatic in her driveway.

I crumpled the twenty bucks in my hand just as the front door flung open and for a scattered heartbeat, I thought she had changed her mind. She'd smile at me, and wave like she always had whenever she caught sight of me. Everything would go back to being our level of normal. The world righted.

But nope.

My world thundered around me like an unexpected storm, launching a lightning bolt straight to my gut.

Chase stood just outside the door. It took him a second to spot me and I sucked in a breath as he sprinted toward my car. The knot in the pit of my stomach replaced the rage. Chase caught my eyes through the windshield and breathing became difficult. Chase was everything I wanted to be. Handsome, bright, *normal*.

And he made me feel sick but not sick. He made everything weird. Weirder than my level of weird. I wanted to be normal for him…like him. I meant like him.

Chase knocked on my window. I lowered it. "Hey, can you give me a ride? I'll pay you."

"Uh, sure?"

He didn't seem to care that I had questioned myself. He sprinted around the front of the car and hopped inside. "Do you know where Liam lives?"

Chase smelled like fresh chocolate chip cookies, peppermint, and weed. The peppermint always on him was supposed to mask the smell of weed. I wanted to tell him it really didn't work. I'm sure his parents knew exactly that he smoked the stuff, just ignored it. The combination made the scent all him. It reminded me of the times I'd spent at his house. Sometimes he'd try to insert himself in whatever Jaylene and I were doing. Whether jolting her feathers when we watched TV by keeping his bedroom door open and playing his guitar until she slammed his door shut in frustration or licking batter from the spoon we used to make chocolate chip cookies so that she and I would have more dishes to wash. I did like watching him lick that spoon.

He snapped his fingers in front of my face, breaking me from my thoughts. "Earth to Jordan, do you know where Liam lives?"

Thankfully, he wasn't a mind reader. "Uh, no."

"Make a right."

He leaned back, running his hands on his thighs, and closed his eyes. His pale throat exposed. Long lashes fanned out on his cheeks. Okay, maybe I saw the appeal

Aimee spoke of. Chase was handsome above the neck too.

"Dude, stop staring and drive."

I snapped to attention and moved the car. "What happened to your truck? Don't tell me you crashed it again." I'd heard plenty of arguments between Chase and his dad regarding that truck.

He growled and shifted again without opening his eyes. Long finger sprayed out on his thighs. "You sound like my parents. Don't need the lecture."

"That was a cue for you to defend yourself. I read that we *humans* become instinctively defensive when accused of something. So, actually, I was just starting a conversation."

"By pissing me off? No wonder you don't have any friends."

Ouch. "I have friends." My voice came out a little too high.

"Aimee is a psych major. You know that, right? And Riley just wants to get into her pants."

"What does her major have to do with anything? And why would Riley want her pants? It's ridiculous."

He laughed. Not the laugh that invited the other person to laugh along. He was laughing *at* me. And it stung. A lot. I don't know why it stung. I shouldn't have had feelings if Vicky had been correct about me missing the day God handed out empathy during my own evolution in my biological mother's womb.

I hated these feelings whenever Chase was around. The uncertainty about everything that made me *me* surfaced whenever he was around me. And this tingling that started at my core and spread throughout my body whenever he looked my way. Tingles. Oh, shit. I had tingles! What did that mean? That had to mean something.

It means Vicky lied to you. You don't lack the emotions needed to be normal. You're just a freak by default.

I stiffened at the voice in my head. I hated that voice. I kept my eyes on the road.

That creepy feeling of being watched lifted the hairs at the back of my neck. He fell silent and I could tell he was looking at me. I didn't want him to see me with feelings.

"I'm sorry, man," he finally said. "I'm just being an asshole."

"I don't remember you being such an asshole to *me*."

"Yeah, well everyone changes."

"Do we?" I asked, sounding so damn hopeful. "Do you think *I* can change? Be normal?"

He looked at me as if trying to figure something out. I'd seen that look on him when he was trying to anticipate an opponent's move on the basketball court. I wanted to look more, but I had to drive.

"Yeah, Jordan. I think you can change to be as normal as you want," he said, dryly as if being normal wasn't something to strive for.

"What's wrong with trying to be normal?"

He snorted, shifting in his seat again and spreading his thighs apart. It made me realize how much taller and bigger he was than me. "Normal is fake. Do you want to be a fake person?"

"Yes," I blurted. I couldn't be the real me. His eyes opened and he slid them my way. Thankfully, I didn't get the full extent of that look since I was paying attention to the road. "No?" I amended. Now I was confused.

"Are you hurting anyone, Jordan?" The curt sound of my name made me sit up straighter.

"No," I snapped. "I'd never hurt anyone. Why would you ask such a thing?"

Liar. The voice in my head said. I ignored that voice.

"Are you hurting yourself?"

"No. What's this got—"

"Then there's nothing wrong with you," he said over my words. "Stop saying you're not normal, and you'll be normal."

I opened my mouth and snapped it closed before something stupid launched out of it. "So, is this like the power of the universe manifesting your desires?"

He shrugged. His leather sounded like Velcro against the vinyl seat. "I don't know about the universe, but I think if someone tells you something enough times, you start to believe it's true when it's not."

"The power of suggestion. I know that one."

"Right. Your *friend* is a psych major."

I didn't like the way he said *friend*. "What do you have against Aimee?"

"Nothing."

"That didn't sound like nothing."

He sighed. "It's nothing, Jordan."

The bristle in his voice made me stop asking questions. Chase had never been this prickly with me. Not whenever we'd been alone. Something changed between us.

Jaylene. He was only nice to you for his sister.

I bit my bottom lip hard just to keep from blurting out that question.

He instructed me where to turn and we ended up driving along a gravel driveway into one of the largest ranches on this side of town. "Wow, I should've known."

"Known what?" he demanded.

"That Liam was rich like you."

"What's that supposed to mean?"

"You don't slum," I said, dragging my eyes away from the super big house back to him when I stopped the car. "Unless you need something. Like a ride." I smiled because it was better than a scowl. He did not smile back. Apparently, he preferred the scowl.

"Is it just *me o*r do you think Jay was slumming too when she chose to be friends with you?"

By the sound of his voice, I knew I shouldn't have answered that question. "I think she wanted someone she could control, and I gave that to her until I said no to being her boyfriend. Then she didn't want to slum anymore and found cleaner waters with Finn."

"And you think I'm like that?"

"I think if you didn't need a ride, you wouldn't have talked to me all school year."

Chase looked like he wanted to murder me. "Wow, at least you're honest." He got out of the car and tossed in some bills. "Here's some money. Looks like you need it."

Double ouch because it was true.

He slammed the door hard, then sprinted behind the house.

Why did it suddenly feel as if I'd broken up with Chase? I rubbed my chest at the subtle hurt I felt there.

Ugh, the Coopers were all assholes.

I started to leave when a large pale Labrador stopped in front of the car. Thankfully, Hector stopped better than he did forward motion. The dog looked at me, tail wagging as if unsure what he should do next.

I liked dogs. I had one when I was a kid. I think. I couldn't really remember. I rolled down my window and stuck my head out.

"Excuse me, *Dog*," I said. "Can you move out of the way? You're kinda blocking the road."

The dog cocked his head but didn't move. At least not for several seconds. He must've heard something because he sprinted behind Chase.

"Thank you!" I called out the window as I rolled passed him.

He didn't turn back.

Chapter Five

I drove to Harris Funeral Home and Cremation Services, a bit guilty and a bit angry at the whole day.

"Anger sucks your soul out of your body. It is not worth it," I muttered Vicky's words.

For everything that made her life hard, she simply said the emotion wasn't worth it. Love thy neighbor who refuses to clean the snow. Not worth it. Feel guilty for things out of your control. Double not worth it. I figured Vicky had a lot of miles with the *not worth it* feeling.

I stopped by the side of the road and picked some wildflowers. They smelled nice and would die in a few weeks anyway when the cold landed in this part of the world. By the time I got to work, my anger had dissipated to a low throb just behind my eyeballs.

Mr. Harris was in the office while Mrs. Harris was putting the finishing touches on Mrs. Wyman's arrangement. I knew Mrs. Wyman. Her husband, Ernest Wyman, owned the food mart close to the funeral home. It's where I'd purchase the supplies for the families who used our services. Water, juice, and snacks. Little Timmy Wyman always helped me carry the bundles to the truck inquiring about the dead people we'd embalmed—though I never embalmed the body. I needed a degree to do that. Mr. Harris did all the prep work while I assisted. Mrs. Wyman died of a blood clot to the brain. She still looked like herself in death. Sweet and beautiful. Life had been kind to her.

The Harrises were a married couple who owned and ran the funeral service which had switched from generation to generation for a hundred years, according to Mr. Harris. A big black man that reminded me of the

Kingpin if the Kingpin lost a bit more weight. Mrs. Harris stood half his size, maybe a little more. She always made him healthy foods. I didn't know why he was so big.

Mr. Harris looked at the wildflowers bunched in my hand.

"I pulled these from the side of the road on my way over here. Thought Mrs. Wyman would like them."

Mr. Harris arched a brow. Yeah, I knew she was dead, and I knew he knew I knew she was dead. But until they were buried or cremated, I felt as if they were still around. Still lingering. Though I couldn't see them.

"Mrs. Harris is with her if you want to give them to her."

I nodded and walked toward the first viewing room. The family would be in tomorrow and Mrs. Wyman would be buried at Our Lady of Sorrows Cemetery a day later. Mrs. Harris smiled at the flowers.

"Oh, these are perfect. You're so sweet, Jordan."

I felt something stir inside my chest at her kind words but quickly buried it. I wouldn't know what to do with praise, though I heard it in her voice. It made me uncomfortable. "What would you like me to do?" I asked.

"Can you get the back room ready for tomorrow? We need some supplies."

Meant going into town to get them since Mr. Wyman's store was closed due to his wife being dead and all. I nodded and stopped by Mr. Harris's office. He was signing papers and clicking on the keyboard with one finger. "You really should get an accountant," I said.

"Nah, I can handle these."

"It takes you forever to do them."

"I have more than enough time." He peered around the monitor at me. His brown eyes speared me, and I suddenly felt the possibility that *he* could see into my soul. "I heard something about Mrs. Mulcahy. Do you want to tell me what happened?"

The town was too small.

I could've lied and told him Mrs. Mulcahy was not in her right mind. She wasn't. She lived with that demon cat in that old creepy house in the middle of the woods. Sure, I lived in a creepy house in the woods too, but whatever. I'd never lied to Mr. Harris before. I couldn't recall ever lying to anyone. That would have to change as soon as I decided if I wanted to be normal. Normal people lied all the time. "She caught me burying a woodrat and thought it was Mrs. Tubbs."

His arched brow didn't lower.

"It was the third critter I buried in her property this week," I said and flopped on the chair in front of the desk. I didn't mention the other thirteen.

"She didn't ask you to bury them?" Mr. Harris asked.

I shook my head, keeping my eyes on my hands. "I couldn't help it. I couldn't just leave them there."

"You are a good kid, Jordan. Do you know that?"

I looked at him and scratched my nose. Praise made me itchy.

"You see things. You know things. You're honest about things. Not everyone can see that about you."

"Sheriff says I have to be normal, even if I have to fake it."

Mr. Harris made a noise. "You are normal, son."

"I've never kissed a girl," I blurted, thinking about Jaylene. "I'm sixteen and I had a beautiful girl ask me to be her boyfriend. I said no. I've never had an erection and my friend at school says that's not normal." I looked up to see Mr. Harris's cheeks turn a deep red. "Am I making you uncomfortable? Is it not normal to talk about these things?"

Now he scratched his nose. "You usually should

talk to your father about these things."

"I don't know him."

"I know. And I want you to talk to me, but I'm an old man. I haven't had your problem in over forty years."

I snorted. "I don't think you'd ever had my problems." I could give him a list.

"Son, every man has had your problem. Every young man is different."

"Yeah, but I'm *really* different."

Mr. Harris smiled. It was big and genuine. I liked his smile mainly because he rarely wore it. Especially in his profession. "You'll figure it out. The important thing is to be safe."

"You mean, like, use a condom and stuff?"

He nodded, his eyes going back to the monitor. "Hmm, mmm." I knew he was getting uncomfortable.

"Am I weird for not feeling weird talking about it? I mean, arousal is a biological response. Humans are the only species to be embarrassed by it."

"Can you get an extra case of water for the house at the store?" Mr. Harris added, clearly concluding my sexual education with him.

Normal? Blah. Homo Sapiens were all weird. I got to my feet. "Yes, sir. Text me if you need anything else."

Twenty minutes later, I ended up at Wally's Mart in aisle ten, staring at the vast array of contraceptives. If I was going to be *normal*, I had to find a way to up my libido, which meant getting laid. Surely, once I crossed that off my male bucket list, Sheriff Johnson would consider me *normal*.

Manufacturers of this particular need were all insane. Too many colors, flavors, and sizes. And for all different actions. My eyes wanted to bleed. I had no fucking clue what was considered safe or what the hell

I'd need.

A man looking at the liquor options near the display I was currently searching through glanced my way, smirked, and glanced back at the booze. Average height, dark hair, old, maybe Vicky's age. He had a holster with a gun at his hip and a badge next to it. A cop of some sort though I didn't recognize him to be one of Sheriff Johnson's. I knew all the deputies in town.

"Any advice for me here?" I asked, gesturing to the rack in front of me.

"Depends on the night you're expecting," he said with that same smirk. "Piña colada vs Krispy Kreme's." He laughed, shaking his head.

I did the same because it seemed so ridiculous. Especially, since I had no clue what I'd do with the flavored stuff. Okay, maybe I did know what I'd do. In theory. But it didn't make it any easier to choose. I reached for the regular size, thin that offered protection and sensitivity. A six pack. I didn't think I'd need more than that.

"Good choice," the man said as he pulled a bottle of vodka off the rack on his side.

"Be safe," I said.

He arched a thick brow. "You too."

I paid with the twenty bucks Chase had shoved on me (thank you Chase) and departed the store with my items plus some Pez candies of different colors. After I dropped everything off, minus my personal items, I headed home. Vicky was already at work.

I dropped my stuff in my room and headed to the bathroom.

Inspecting myself in the mirror, I took in all of me. I stood an inch shorter than average. Dark curly hair that did whatever it wanted. My eyes seemed to be the best and worst feature on my face. They were a touch lighter than sand, hazel and really round on my face. They were also waxy and hazy. Anyone who looked at me knew there was something wrong with me. Madness lingered in the eyes.

I could still hear Chase laughing at me. A cruel laugh that made me feel horrible inside. Wrong somehow. He'd never been that cruel before, but people changed. We all could change. I could change. I could be normal. Like Chase, but not an asshole.

I should talk to Vicky about stopping my meds first. Aimee had been right. I was old enough for patient autonomy and Dr. Cooper probably would've helped wean me off them. But it felt wrong to ask Vicky to take a chance on me. She didn't owe me anything, but I owed her everything. She'd taken me in when she didn't have to. I was still considered returnable. There wasn't an expiration date on handing me back to the group home. I'd done things. Horrible things. I wanted to prove to her I'd be okay without the meds before telling her. I *could* be normal.

"What would Chase do if his medications were affecting his libido?" I asked myself in the mirror. "He'd drop the meds." I opened the medicine cabinet and meticulously replaced my pills with the color coordinating Pez candy and flushed the real thing down the toilet.

I watched as they disappeared and wondered how long it would take for me to decompensate without them. I guess I'd find out tomorrow.

Chapter Six

The human stages of decomposition started with self-digestion with a side order of putrid gasses that stunk up everything and ended with the liquefaction of organic matter which then leaked out of orifices until only bones remained.

The same stages facing me now.

It started with the inability to control my muscles. I felt as if my whole body were on fire, and I couldn't stop my cells from twitching just under my skin. I started to run again just to keep my body in check. I ran for miles every morning before school. It helped with jitteriness so I could sit through classes. Made me too tired to move. Then came dehydration. I felt as if I were being sucked dry. I inhaled water until I vomited and vomited. Between the shaking and the dehydration, I knew if I didn't come clean about my purge of medications I was going to die. Normalcy went out the window along with my sanity.

Sanity. Contemplating your sanity means you're sane.

It hadn't made sense to me before and it sure as hell didn't make sense now. I felt as if I were *dying*. Thankfully, being in love had Vicky distracted. She'd spend nights over with the sheriff after work and woke up late when she was home. Our mornings were a slow-paced tired hello and not much else. Because I was too afraid of dying, I didn't cause any trouble.

Aimee came over a few times to feed me and argue how I'd lost my mind. She wasn't wrong. She brought all her psychology books and seemed quite intrigued by my symptoms. Even wrote a paper about it.

"You should wean off the drugs with your psychiatrist."

I groaned. "Vicky takes me to the free clinic where Dr. Cooper works."

"Jaylene's mother is your psychiatrist?" Aimee hadn't known that. Obviously.

"Yes. That's where I met Jay."

Aimee arched her brow. She hadn't known that either. The Coopers were a private family. I should've known. "You know, because her mom works there." I tried to backtrack rather than saying Jay also saw a therapist.

She glared at me as if she knew I was lying. "You know they study these meds with rats, right?" She quickly changed the subject.

My sludge brain didn't have a response for that.

Aimee shook her head. "Well, I'm no expert, but I think you're screwed."

"I'm dying," I reminded her.

She shrugged this time.

No help.

At least she didn't rat me out. Ha. Ha. Pun intended.

The more it hurt, the more I didn't want to go back to my life before. As if I deserved the hurting part. As if the hurting part had to mean something or I did it for nothing. My mind was a weird place.

I had managed to work despite my symptoms though Mr. and Mrs. Harris sent me home the first couple of days with some soup and order to rest.

Then, one day it stopped hurting. The sweating, the dying of thirst, the cramps, all of it just stopped. I'd boiled my medications from the inside out. I felt less fuzzy in my mind. And…and I woke up with a boner.

An erection!

It tented my PJs.

It worked!

Mission accomplished! My first response was to call Riley but then I thought, what would Chase do? He sure as hell would not tell anyone about his erection. I jumped into the shower with a little bounce and even touched it. A lot. Yeah. It worked.

Today would be a good day!

Vicky was in the kitchen cooking bacon and eggs. She glanced at me over her shoulder with a smile she only wore when Sheriff Johnson was in her room. The only closed door in the house and with a doorknob. The bathroom didn't have a doorknob. We used a tag that said occupied to let us know when it was in use. My room had a curtain to give me privacy. But her room had a doorknob. "Hey, come eat. I want to talk."

I dropped my backpack at the door and sat at the counter. It's where she liked to talk. She slid some eggs and bacon my way. "You look so thin. Are you losing weight?"

Yes, I had lost weight. "I'm just running more now. Getting in shape." Not a lie.

That made her smile. She handed me my pills which I always took after breakfast. Meant she suspected something. I started sweating just on principle. She watched as I swallowed them. "I have to work overnights for a few weeks. It's more money so I volunteered, figured maybe you can go on your senior trip next year."

Guilt was a nasty flavor on my tongue, or maybe it was the Pez. I got up and hugged her. "Woah," she laughed and hugged me back. Every touch against my skin burned. I never hugged but it put a smile on her face. Win. Win. She awkwardly patted my back before I let her go.

"Thanks, I have some saved up too. Maybe together."

"Together," she repeated. "Will you be okay on your own?"

"I'll be fine."

"Well, in case of an emergency, you can get a hold of me at the hospital's main line, but in a real emergency, I want you to call Jack, okay?"

Jack Johnson. That was a stupid name. Sheriff Johnson had once hauled me in on an APB after I missed curfew with Jaylene and Vicky had called him hysterical. Jaylene had gotten a lecture by his team of four officers about the importance of meeting curfew. It hadn't even been Jaylene's fault and she took the blame. In payment, Jaylene had me attend a Supreme Court lecture with her as torture. I never lived it down. "Yeah, I will." *Not.* "How serious is it with you two anyway?" I asked. I preferred to know these things to prepare boundaries.

"Very serious. I think."

"Like getting married serious?"

"Maybe. We haven't really talked about it."

"But sex serious."

She blushed but she was used to my forwardness. "Yes. He's in my bedroom, if that's what you're asking."

"Are you happy?"

She smiled and blushed. "Yeah. I am."

She deserved to be happy. Unfortunately, if Jack Johnson made her happy, I had to tolerate him and his deadbeat son. "Good. That's what it's about, right? Happiness?" This I had no clue. I didn't know what would make *me* happy. Strike that. The erection this morning made me happy. I hoped she'd understand when she found out about my lying ways.

"Yeah," she said. "What about you? Homecoming is coming up. Did you and Jaylene make up yet?"

"No. She's going with Finn now."

Vicky scrunched her face in clear disapproval.

"That harlot," she whispered because she couldn't very well blame Finn, her maybe stepson.

I didn't bother mentioning it had been my decision not to be with her. I wasn't in the mood for a lecture of how perfect Jaylene Cooper was for me. I finished my plate, rinsed it off, and headed for the door.

"Jordan," she said. "Stay safe."

"I will. Promise." I gave her a small wave and took off in my car after a few moments of Hector coughing and growling on the verge of mutiny until he turned on.

Everybody in WS High School knew that Jaylene Cooper had dumped me like a bad record album. It didn't matter that we hadn't *actually* dated. The whispers were the same.

"She dumped him."

"I heard he was caught burying Mrs. Mulcahy's cat alive."

"He's not normal."

Jaylene passed by with Finn without sparing me a glance. Having her in my arms would've upped my popularity meter, that was for sure.

I skulked into first period and took a seat at my assigned seating. Mrs. Brainard preferred to know where every student sat. Creating a familiar space, is what she called it. I didn't mind. I liked order.

"Mr. Cooper," Mrs. Brainard said, looking at someone behind me. "Cap off, please."

I didn't have to turn to know that Chase Cooper took off his UM cap and that his hair was tied up in a messy manbun. Or that his blue eyes were probably spearing the back of my head as he took his assigned seat behind me. My Brooks to his Cooper. Though Chase was a year older than Jaylene and I, he had been held back a grade at the request of his parents, so we were in the same grade. They had wanted him to enter college with his sister. Chase hadn't complained about it. He'd do anything for his sister.

I'd been too sick these last few days to care about the glares he threw my way. Now it's all I thought about. And I realized, after talking to Aimee, that I may have sounded obtuse. I had accused him of being a classist, caring more about money than people. I'd been a big dick and not in a good way.

After class, he sprung out of the room too fast for me to try to talk to him. I'd catch up to him during gym class. I could talk to him while he was in the shower. Sure, why not? I was thinking about that and not about the three assholes following me to the bathroom. Bathroom doors didn't have doorknobs. They had push plates. This particular steel push plate rushed to meet my face as someone slammed me into it from behind. The door swung open hard and slammed into the wall before Trace Asshat closed it behind him. He stood in front of it so no one else could enter. Steel Morrison (yeah, his asshole parents named him Steel) shoved me against the wall hard.

"It's been a while, fuck face," he snapped as if I hadn't heard that before. "Where's my shit?"

"I don't know what you mean." My eyes swept from Trace at the door, Miller behind Steel, and Steel-man himself. I had asked Vicky for boxing lessons once. She said kindness makes the world go round. Not fists. I didn't think it applied to bullies.

"My drugs, asshole. I'm sure someone as pathetic as you could spare."

Maybe this scenario had been my fault. Vicky had celebrated a birthday a few months ago and I had wanted to buy her a nice gift but hadn't had enough funds and found a willing idiot to buy some pills off of me. I'd turned into a sporadic dealer after that, not by choice. Obviously. Had I thought about sharing, I would've sold him the stash I had flushed two weeks ago or given it to him if I knew it'd save me a beating. "I don't have any. I'm weaned off."

That earned me a slap to the face hard enough to sting. His ring—which I'm sure he wore for this reason—sliced my lip at the corner. I tasted blood. Steel wasn't a puncher. He was a slapper. Not sure if I'd survive a punch. "Well, good for fucking you. I'm sure you can convince some dipshit to give you more. Tomorrow." With another round of slaps from the creepoids behind him, they all marched out.

I steadied my breathing and clung to the sink, my face burning. I had to admit I thought of the many ways I could kill them. A knife, poison, shoving them in a vat of acid. Tears inevitably made an appearance, and I splashed water on my face before heading to gym class. By that time, I was already late, and the hallways were empty. It always felt creepy how the hallways could be full of people one second, then totally empty the next. Though the sounds of footsteps lingered as if ghosts took to the halls at that precise moment. And all the doors were closed.

I didn't have a problem with closed doors. I was fine with bathroom stalls that didn't reach the floor or ceiling. I didn't have a problem with the classroom doors because they had windows you could look through. I didn't have a problem with the exit doors as they too had a push plate. A different kind of push plate, but not a doorknob. Yeah, my problem doors were all solid with a freaking doorknob like the one leading to the boy's locker room.

They say that the healing process starts by admitting you have a problem. I admitted I had a problem since I was six. Admitting did shit for me. The meds had done shit for me. Or strike that. They made mc numb so I wouldn't care as much. But it was always there. A sliding shadow across my brain telling me to run.

As I stood stock still two feet away from the door, staring at the dark finish, the faded gloss, the silver knob, I couldn't breathe. The world at my peripheral's turned to dark shadows. The seam of the door pulsed, and the light underneath spilled a blood line just in front of it.

Then the screams started.

High pitched, terror filled screams.

Breathe. Breathe. In and out. In and out.

Something slammed against the door, forcing it to bulge under the strain. The doorknob turned, left and right, but it didn't open.

Another scream.

A woman.

Breathe. Breathe. I clenched my fists until my nails dug into my palms. My body turned cold as if I'd been dipped in cold water.

Then my vision narrowed, and I plunged into darkness.

Chapter Seven

I woke up to a familiar face. Blue-gray eyes rimmed with black liner, a perfect nose, a chin with the first dusting of a beard, full lips, and hair tucked into a black beanie. My handsome prince.

Then he slapped me.

"Ow," I hissed. The slap wasn't hard, but I'd already had my slap allotment for the day.

"Get up. You're in the middle of the hallway."

I was sprawled on the floor. The dirty, icky floor with hundreds of foot traffic a day, not including the ghosts. Chase helped me to my wobbly feet and even held me for a little bit. We were so close I couldn't help but to lean into him and inhale his scent. He smelled of the same peppermint and weed. Surprisingly, not unpleasant.

"You okay? What happened?"

It took me a moment to realize he was cupping my face. His thumb gently slid along my busted bottom lip. Before I could say something cool, like I slammed my face with a door, I said, "Steel slapped me." I sounded like a big baby.

The expression that slid across Chase's face bordered on homicidal. Something the prince of hell would wear. Chase didn't ask any more questions. He turned to the door, then back to me. He shook his head as if clearing his thoughts and reached for the door.

"Don't," I blurted.

"It's okay, Jordan," he said, his voice full of kindness. The opposite of the storm raging in his eyes.

Throughout the years at his house whenever I stood facing a door, he'd always tell me the same thing.

51

It's okay. It's okay. I wanted to believe it was okay. I couldn't. The woman was screaming beyond the door. Something horrible was happening to her. I couldn't get the words out as Chase turned the knob and pushed the door open. The shadows beyond lifted, cleared, and nothing but a long stretch of hallway leading into the locker room unfolded beyond. I'd been down that hallway countless times, except never late. Never with the door closed.

"Come on," he said, kindly.

I walked in first. As I got to the turn, my heart already slowed, my mind already in the now, and I shakily made it to my locker to change.

After that, Chase avoided me as always. Mr. Jenkins, the coach, usually ignored the scrawny nonathletic kids and allowed the others to have a game. We, the lower end of the coordinated gene pool, would get only a few minutes of playing time just to get a passable grade.

I watched Chase move up and down the court with the basketball. Sweaty Chase looked my way, and my body suddenly came alive. Like vibrating with something I'd never felt before. Something deep. I remembered Chase touching my face, the warmth of his hands on my cool skin, how his eyes lowered to my lips, and I couldn't help but to look down at my—

"Brooks!"

Startled, I got to my feet. "Yes, I'm here." I squealed with my hand raised up in the air like an idiot.

Most of the people on the court snickered my way, even Chase.

"Yes, I see that," Coach said. "You can put your hand down now."

I did. Even the nonathletics chuckled at me. Nice to know where I fell among them too.

"Get in with the blue."

Crap. I took the blue smock from Reece. "Good luck," he said. It was more like a warning.

I pulled the thing over my head and secured it around my waist trying not to think of the sweat already on it. Ew...I needed a hot scrub. The whistle blew before I could ask what the hell I was supposed to do, and a crowd of guys ran my way. A very determined Chase with the ball in the lead.

I froze.

He slammed into me, and I fell on my ass, covering my head to make sure no one stepped on my brain as I went down.

The coach blew the whistle. "Come on, Cooper," Coach admonished. "You know better than that."

Liam helped me up with a broad smile on his face. He was also blue. "Good job, squirt," he said and slapped my butt. Coach threw me the ball.

"You got two shots, Brooks. Make them count."

Chase speared me with a look that reminded me of evil incarnate as Liam pointed where I needed to stand to make the shot. "We have three seconds on the clock. You make it in twice, we win. No pressure." He gave me a wink. His eyes lowered to my lip and the space between his brows folded as if he wanted to ask me about it. He didn't.

"Hurry up, Brooks," Coach said.

I dribbled the ball, feeling the coarse rubber texture of the skin on my fingertips, then picked it up like I'd seen Chase do countless times. One hand on the bottom, the other just above. I flicked my wrist pushing the ball into the air in a perfect arc.

Whoosh. The ball went in. All net.

Liam gave me a high five. He seemed the only one on the court happy for me. "Go again," he said, and slapped my ass. Again. I kind of liked it. Chase scowled at me.

I started to line the shot when Chase lifted the hem of his shirt to wipe his face. Thick corded abs visible until he dropped the shirt. Heat sifted up my neck to gather on my cheeks. I had to turn back to focus on the hoop and ball before I internally combusted. This is easy. Neanderthal easy. Ball in hoop. I dribbled, set up, and shot it. This time it bounced off the rim before whooshing inside the net.

The blue team busted in applause led by Liam. "Good job, Brooks," Liam said and gave me another butt slap.

Coach called us all to the locker room.

I got good jobs from the blue team and snickers from the red team. Nothing from Chase. He simply acted as if I didn't exist. I guess it was better than the sneers he threw my way. It reminded me that I had to apologize to him for calling him a classist prick and thank him for plucking me off the hallway floor.

I dressed hurriedly in my faded jeans, black Star Wars t-shirt, and converse hoping to meet Chase before he left. I realized I didn't have to hurry. He was waiting for me at the end of the hall before the door. I caught sight of him before he saw me. Leaning against the wall, one leg propped up on it, eyes closed, hands in his hoodie pocket. His throat exposed.

Get a grip, Jordan.

Being unmedicated was really doing something to my body whenever Chase was around. I didn't like it because I had no control. I felt as if I were falling and hadn't quite reached the ground yet. Although we were the only two in the locker room right now, he must've felt me staring because he pushed himself off the wall and turned to me.

For a moment, the world didn't exist. Just us. Me and him. I wished I could read his mind, or his expression, but he didn't give anything away. Except when his eyes lowered to my lips and his nostrils flared. I felt the need to say something.

"I'm sorry," I said.

He seemed taken aback. "For what?"

"For what I said. I don't really think you're a classist asshole."

He shrugged as if it hadn't been on his mind like it had been on mine. "You have your moments. I get it."

Moments. Like crazy moments. He plopped me into a label, a sidenote, broken. Who the hell was I kidding? I could never be normal. Angry, I brushed past him and stopped at the closed door. Why was the door closed? My IEP specifically stated that doors with knobs had to be left open.

The screams.

I took a step back right into Chase. His arms instinctively wrapped around me, his chin just above my shoulder. "People are being dicks to you because of Jay."

I felt his breath at my neck, his lips near my ear. It sent shivers rushing through me. Because of the door. Not him. Not because of him. But I didn't hear the screams anymore and I didn't want to move away from him. He moved away first and propped the door open for me with the door stopper. He glanced back at my lips, because he didn't meet my eyes, and walked away into the crowd.

My savior, the prince of hell.

ELIZABETH ARROYO

Chapter Eight

"That's a horrible idea."

Aimee scrunched her brow at me. "She's pretty."

Riley rolled his eyes and Aimee elbowed his ribs. He wasn't fast enough to protect himself and flinched. I wondered where love played in all this contact. Deciding not to ask, I took a bite of my hotdog instead and Riley loudly sucked on his straw.

"Well, who are you going to go to homecoming with?" she asked.

I shrugged. "Not pretty Penny."

Riley choked on his soda on a laugh and coughed. "Good one, dude," he said, and we bumped fists.

"So, you're missing homecoming. That is *not* normal."

"Ouch," Riley said. "Hit the poor dude below the belt."

She shrugged. She also wasn't wrong. Even Vicky had been excited when I told her about homecoming, and she said she'd pay for it. I sucked on my straw just to think, hoping Riley would say something to distract us both.

"She's right, dude," he said instead. "You should go."

Uh, Riley, being serious was like listening to Mr. Harris's lectures. I couldn't help but to take them at face value because it made sense. Mostly. "Fine," I rolled my eyes. "Does she really want to go with me?"

Aimee's smile widened. "Yeah, she's been crushing on you since sophomore year."

Riley made a face making me believe there was something else about this crush I should know. "You're off your meds, right?"

That earned him another elbow torture from his girlfriend.

I ignored his loaded question. "What does one wear to these things?"

Aimee opened her mouth, but Riley beat her to it. "Don't listen to girls on fashion, dude. Definitely not normal."

He averted the elbow by quickly anticipating it and moving away.

"Anyway," Aimee said, leaning further into the table as if starting a secret. Matt's Diner was packed today. Most of the students were enjoying Hotdog Friday before we went home. Despite all the other conversations going on around the restaurant, someone would pick up on her secret. Some people were just wired that way. "Did you hear about the body?"

Riley stopped sucking his straw to pay attention which made me do the same. Aimee's dad was a Chief Deputy and second to the sheriff. While I avoided the sheriff at all costs, apparently, she didn't avoid her father, nor the adult conversations floating around her house about a body.

"They found her near Miller's Creek."

"Shit, isn't that near your house?" Riley asked, looking at me.

Miller's Creek lay three miles from my house, the opposite way of the school. "Everything remote is near my house," I said. True. My house bordered with nature on all four sides. At night it was creepy, so Vicky had set up lights along our driveway and backyard. Sometimes we got critters in our garbage and one time even a bear. Vicky had freaked and called the sheriff. The great big bear attack. Though the bear hadn't attacked and went leisurely on its way. Vicky and I had gotten instructions on what not to do when faced with a bear. Do not scream. Do not run. Ignore all your survival instincts and slowly move away.

"How'd she die?" Riley asked with nervous tension in his voice.

"They don't know yet, but it's a *criminal* investigation right now, so—"

"Murder. Someone killed her." Riley didn't have to state the obvious. "Wow, that sucks. Did your dad ground you yet?"

I had to blink away my ears. "A girl is dead, and you're worried about her being grounded?"

He shrugged.

"And you consider me *not* normal?"

"Okay, Hannibal, what were you thinking then?" Riley challenged me. He did that a lot. As if he wanted to get into my psycho brain.

"I was actually thinking about a bear that once attacked me and Vicky," I said. "And maybe if Mr. Harris will get the body."

He pointed at me with a smile. "See, diabolical."

Aimee rolled her eyes. "You two are both crazy."

"Watch it, sweetheart," Riley said. "We don't use the word *crazy* in front of crazy people."

He glared at me. I gave him my long middle finger.

Aimee got to her feet. "Well, I'm outta here."

Riley got to his feet. "Wait, but—"

That's as far as I heard as he scurried out behind her. Yes, he left his trash. I collected it all onto a tray and dumped it. Just as I made my way out, Chase walked in with Tabatha and a couple of his bandmates. Not the first time I'd seen Chase around since my apology, but the first time I wanted to stare at him. Would a normal guy stare at another guy? Nope. Even I knew the answer to that question.

Except at that moment, Steel et al walked in behind Chase.

Fuck. What would a normal me do?

Steel met my eyes and a slow smirk made him look like some sort of serial killer. Chase forgotten. The whole world forgotten. Self-preservation took front and center. Except Steel didn't move away from the exit. He blocked it.

Before I could move to place a table between us, he linked an arm around mine, shoving me into a bench seat and forcing me to scoot over so he could sit beside me and block my escape.

"Hey, Jordan. I missed you in school these last couple days."

I pressed myself as far away from him as I could. Not far enough. His goons smiled with their crooked lips and pockmarked faces. "I told you," I said. "I don't have anything for you."

"Oh, come on. I'm sure we can make an arrangement."

I shook my head. "I can't."

Trace ripped my backpack from my hands and started looking through it. My heart about wretched itself out of my throat when he pulled out my small notebook. "What's this?" he lifted his eyes to me, and I reached across the table for it, but Steel yanked on my collar, choking me back into sitting beside him.

"Stop. Give it back."

Trace slid it to Steel who opened my action lists. His eyes gleamed as if he'd been given the best Christmas gift in the universe. And he read the passage out loud. The restaurant seemed to silence all in one sweep. "How to be normal," he said with a smile I wanted to stab with a fork. "Stop meds equals increased libido. Aw, does baby Brooks have an erectile dysfunction disorder? Can't get it up?"

The blood drained from my body.

Steel threw his head back and laughed. The world around me shifted into a monochromatic gray. The voices of the people around us became muffled. The pulsing in my head intensified. Something dark soared through me and I stabbed Steel in the carotid with my fork. Blood squirted out of the wound as his face drained of color. The voices around me exploded louder.

Jordan is a killer. Jordan is a killer. K.I.L.L.E.R.

With a jolt, the world snapped back into color. The dark stain lifted, yanked out of me in a sudden move that left me unable to suck in air. Steel wasn't bleeding, and I wasn't a killer. He was still laughing loud enough to draw attention and I felt the sudden need to spew what I'd just eaten. The singsong voice of someone in my head said over and over. *Jordan is a killer. Jordan is a killer. K.I.L.L.E.R.*

My head was going to pop any minute now.

I clenched my hands into tight fists when a shadow forced my eyes to Chase glaring at Steel as he continued to flip through the pages. Getting close to the section that no one was supposed to see. I held my breath waiting for that moment when all my lies landed on Steel's plate. But Chase yanked the notebook out of Steel's hand before he got there.

"Enough," Chase ordered.

His voice carried more than Steel's, but they warred for control of the situation. I couldn't seem to draw a breath. But then Liam stepped up beside Chase, glaring at the two across from me. "Why don't you fuckers try something with us?"

The question asked of bullies throughout time immemorial. Why beat the little guy when big guys fought better?

Steel's smile turned to steel, but he consented. Lifting his hands up. "Just having fun. That's all."

"Well, go jack off next time," Liam added while Chase just glared at *me*. Me. As if this were somehow my fault.

Or, he'd seen. He'd seen what Steel had been about to see. Oh, God. I wanted to die. "I'd like to leave now," I said without looking at anyone.

Steel scooted out and I rushed outside, my backpack in my clenched fist. I managed to make it to Hector on wobbly legs. I opened the door when Chase came up behind me and slammed the door shut. I spun quickly around with a gasp.

"You forgot something." His voice was sharp enough to cut glass. The notebook lay in his outstretched hand.

I took it. Then he did something I didn't expect. His warm fingers touched my chin and forced me to look at him. He looked worried about me. "Are you okay?"

I nodded. Not okay at all.

"If those assholes ever confront you again, you tell me."

Not what I expected him to say or do. Maybe he hadn't seen it. It took all my will to move away from his fingers. But I did. "I don't need your pity." I actually did. And his muscles and friends that could protect me. But pride got in the way. And something else I couldn't make sense of. This floating, bubbly feeling in the pit of my stomach.

"What do you need from me then?" he asked, losing the sharp edge to his voice.

I couldn't help but to meet his blue-gray eyes. They were curious but full of something, something maybe a normal person would be able to decipher while I just felt my heartbeat pounding hard against my chest as if ready to pop free.

I should've just told him nothing. I didn't need anything from him. Nothing. Nada. Zippo. But my mind and heart usually didn't coincide. "You can help me be normal."

The door to the café opened and Tabatha caught sight of us. "Babe, come on. Food's getting cold."

I shook my head. "Forget it."

I climbed into my car seeking the safety of the enclosure and ignored Chase as he turned and followed his girlfriend inside.

Idiot. I was such an idiot.

"You can help me be normal." What a stupid thing to say. I was so dumb. I should've kept my mouth shut. I shoved the notebook under my thigh just as a knock on my window startled me into a yelp. Liam stood just outside as I lowered my window. "Can we talk?"

"Uh, sure?"

He sprinted around the car and got inside. He stood about the same height as Chase and filled the car almost the same. Except he smelled of musk. Not peppermint. I liked peppermint better.

Without the meds, I'd been trying to identify the feelings vibrating through me. I've been numb for so long that even the brush of cool air against my skin made me itchy. I would've peeled my skin right off if that were normal. And the truth, I preferred it to feeling numb. I drove and Liam's pouty lips moved. They were pink and I wondered if he painted them. His tongue flicked out a lot to wet his lips as he talked about the dead girl. Shit. The dead girl.

"Are you listening?"

Nope. I totally spazzed out. "I don't know anything. Aimee just told me."

"What about the sheriff? Isn't he banging your mother?"

I thought I should defend Vicky's honor, but Liam wasn't wrong. "I'm usually not there when they bang, so I don't know anything." He gave me a weird look. His eyes were a pretty blue, like a clear ocean, framed in long thick lashes. I blinked away the staring. "Did you know her?"

He leaned back, pressed his fingertips to his eyes. "No, not really."

"Then why do you care?"

Cold eyes turned back to me. They were still pretty. "A girl is dead. You'd have to be a monster not to care." He kept looking at me as if trying to see the monster inside of me.

I shifted uncomfortably in my seat, trying to push the monster me back. Did I have a monster inside of me? I had wanted to stab Steel with my fork. I had seen it happen. All the blood included, and I had felt nothing.

"Hey." Liam snapped his fingers in front of my face.

I blinked away the monster thoughts and planted myself in the present. "If I find out anything, I'll let you know," I said, figuring that's what he wanted to hear. I was right when he let out a relieved breath.

"Really?" He sounded hopeful. And I really wanted to be a good friend. Not that Liam was my friend. He was Chase's friend. I hardly knew him at all.

I nodded.

"Thanks. Can you take me back?"

I slammed on the brakes. "Really?" I didn't hide the shock value in my voice. He smiled. It was a nice smile.

"I didn't tell you I wanted a ride. I wanted to talk."

"You could've said that before I moved." I drove him back to the diner and parked in front, overlooking the windows. He turned to me, leaning into my space. For a second, I thought he meant to kiss me. But he plucked a pencil off my visor. "Can I borrow this?"

"Yeah, sure."

"Thanks. You're cute, you know that?" His eyes lowered to my lips and something warm settled in my stomach, then he dragged his eyes back to my eyes. "You remind me of someone."

"Uh, okay."

He tapped the pencil against his knee. "You have a cell phone?"

"Yeah."

"Well, can I have your number? You can call me if you find some news."

Right. On the dead girl. I unlocked my phone and handed it to him. He added his number and texted himself. Then saved my contact.

"Thanks," he said and sprinted back to the diner. I caught Chase watching me through the window. Chase who now probably knew what I'd drawn in my notebook.

Circles, Jordan.

Just circles.

Chapter Nine

News of the dead body hit the TV that night. Vicky was curled up on the sofa, watching the newscast before she went to work. I sat on the floor doing homework. I didn't have a desk. The floor worked just fine.

"I don't want you going out," she finally said. "And keep your phone close, okay?"

"I have to go to school. And I have to work."

She sighed. "Right. Okay, then check in."

"You won't see the text until hours later anyway."

"I still want to see it, Jordan. Just every few hours. Don't make me have to put Finn on you. I will."

That made me want to barf. "Yeah, okay. I will. Except when I'm sleeping."

That made her smile for some reason. "I love you, kiddo."

"I know," I said. I couldn't return the word because I didn't know what it meant. She kissed the top of my head and used it as leverage to get to her feet.

"I have to get ready for work. Text me before you go to bed, okay."

"Okay."

"I'll see you in the morning."

I watched as she disappeared through the closed door. My chest clenched at the memory of the screams in my head. Just in my head. Normal Chase wouldn't hear screams. There were no screams beyond the door. There was nothing beyond the door but shadows.

Mr. Harris was hired to do the funeral arrangements for the dead girl, and we went to the sheriff's office to pick up the body the following week. I hated the sheriff's office. I always felt as if one of the officers was going to charge me with something and arrest me. I made sure to keep clear of them which always led me to the missing person's wall. There were so many. Like a shrine of the most vulnerable. Like me. Kids, younger. Pictures of a time when they'd been happy. Smiling and proud. The best moments of their lives staring back at strangers bearing wilting hearts at the unfairness of the thought of something happening to them. I wondered if their parents were still looking for them. If they still wore those smiles wherever they were. I wondered if anyone bothered to take down their pictures once they were found alive or dead. I searched the board for myself. Not sure why.

A memory tugged at my mind like a tether to wherever the forgotten ones go. Not quite breaking free. Like looking at a horribly exposed photo trying to make out distinct features of the person it's supposed to memorialize. In time, it fades. Or it just doesn't seem worth trying to think about anymore. I stopped trying to find it. It went missing, like the children on the wall.

A familiar man stopped beside me, looking at the board too. Not one of the cops I knew under Sheriff Johnson. I knew all of them. This man held a certain shadow around him. As if he'd seen way too much any one person should. As if he held the woes of the world on his shoulders. As if he needed a drink.

Then it clicked.

The man I'd seen at Wally's Mart when I'd been looking for condoms. Among other supplies. His eyes slowly studied each individual image as if downloading all of them into his brain.

I turned back to the wall. "There's so many of them," I said.

"There are more."

I could imagine a building loaded with discarded flyers of bright young faces. Pictures taken when they were happy. "Do you ever find them?"

"Some," he answered.

"Alive?"

"Some."

We stared at the wall for a few more minutes before we were interrupted. "Special Agent Martinez?"

The man turned slightly to look at Deputy Chief Sloane. I'd never met Aimee's mom. She died a long time ago. But I figured Aimee took after her since she looked nothing like Sloane. The man stood average, with russet colored hair and blue eyes with freckles on the bridge of his nose. Sloane looked at me. "Jordan," he said. "Are you here for the sheriff?"

"No, sir," I said. "I'm here for the body." The apparent confused expression he wore had me explaining that Mr. Harris would be organizing the funeral arrangements. "Mr. Harris is with the sheriff now."

Sloane nodded but kept that suspicious look on me. He knew Aimee and I were friends and didn't particularly like me. "When is the funeral?"

Mrs. Montenegro didn't request a private funeral, which meant the information for the service was online. It meant I wasn't breaking anything confidential and so I told Deputy Chief Sloane when the service would be held. Then I added that he could find all up to date details on the Harris Funeral and Cremation Services website as Mrs. Harris was diligent in updating it accordingly.

Deputy Chief smirked at me. Special Agent Martinez placed a strong hand on my shoulder and squeezed. "Thanks for the information. You let Mr. Harris know we'll be there."

I flinched at the contact but didn't move away. I suddenly felt too small under his sharp gaze. I planted a forced smile on my face instead of pulling sharply away. "Yes, sir."

Special Agent Martinez released his hold and turned his attention to Deputy Chief Sloane. "We have a hit," Sloane said. "We should move."

Sloane didn't wait for Martinez to follow. After giving one glance back at the board, Martinez seemed to turn to stone. "Be safe, kid," he said. Voice rough around the edges.

"Yes, sir," I said. "And thank you for trying."

Not sure why I added that bit. Perhaps, Special Agent Martinez needed to hear that. It at least made the man look at me. Like, really look. Our eyes held for several seconds before he turned away and disappeared wherever Sloane had gone.

I let out a relieved breath.

"Idiot," I muttered. I was an idiot.

Thankfully, Mr. Harris took that moment to walk out with Sheriff Johnson at his heels. "Jordan," Johnson said with a slight nod. He looked worse for wear. A dead body would probably do that to you.

Mr. Harris handed me the paperwork and I shoved it into my sling bag. I helped him secure the body in the van and Mr. Harris drove back to the funeral home where we would prep the body for burial. I knew the girl as Natalia Montenegro. A twenty-one-year-old Hispanic lady. She went missing from UM three months ago and her body was found in Miller's Creek by poor Timmy Wyman while he'd been flyfishing with his grandfather.

Sucked.

"Maybe you should sit this one out," Mr. Harris said, breaking me from my thoughts.

"Why?"

"She was young. Too young."

"Not too young to die," I deadpanned.

Where Vicky would've probably scolded me for being so crass and insensitive, Mr. Harris snorted. Mr. Harris had been hesitant to take me under his wing despite my begging to work for him. I did it for free until I proved that dead bodies didn't scare me. Although I couldn't do the real work, I assisted in what was legal for me.

"You are right about that, son," he said.

The Harrises believed in souls and the afterlife. *The body is a temporary vessel, nothing more. It should be taken care of and respected upon death, having serve its purpose. A family should be given care and consideration to grieve the way they see fit.*

I wasn't so sure about the afterlife or souls. That required having faith and that was something I didn't trust in. I did, however, trust Mr. Harris. It had taken me a while to break my idea of how morticians were creepy dudes. Mr. Harris was nothing like that. He had a wife he'd been married to for thirty years. He'd told me that his great-great grandfather had opened the funeral home. It'd been in the family business for a hundred years. Of course, I had dug the blade deeper and asked him if he intended on having kids to keep the tradition moving on with his kids.

Mr. Harris had gone quiet, her expression reminiscent of those I had seen when people mourned the death of a loved one. The death of kids was always worse, and we didn't charge for the service. Families paid at cost. Something about making money out of the death of babies was quite unsettling.

"My son died when he was very young," he said.

"Why didn't you have another one?"

Mr. Harris had gone tight-lipped and red-faced when he had turned to me. I had asked the wrong question. After a few long breaths, Mr. Harris clapped me on the shoulder. "There's something that scares a person, son," he said, not unkindly. "A fear that pushes your soul to the precipice of darkness. Losing a child does that to a parent. By the time Mrs. Harris and I were well enough to think about having another one, we got old. Decided it best to let things work out on their own." He clapped me twice on the shoulder and then put me to clean the catch basin under the workstations.

Once we reached the funeral home, Mr. Harris backed up the van into the loading area and we moved the body inside. We helped each other into our PEP equipment, then removed the body from the bag and carefully lifted it onto the steel worktable.

The first few times I worked with him in prep work, he'd asked me all sorts of aftercare questions. Like how I felt about the body, about the nakedness. All of it seemed to be some sort of test. I had been honest. I'd never been ashamed of my own body nor the naked body of others. Everyone had the same bits and pieces, inside and out. Everyone lived. Everyone died. Mr. Harris had seemed satisfied with my answers.

I didn't tell him I didn't feel anything for the dead because that wasn't entirely true. I was curious. I wanted to learn about the person in life. Somehow, my brain wanted to reconcile that in their death. I'd started to add personal touches to the service, like Mrs. Wyman's flowers. Somehow knowing that I'd taken care of their family, of them, during their last moments on the surface made me feel as if they left this place happy.

It made me feel as if I were doing something worthwhile.

Mr. Harris went on to double check vitals. Yeah, stories of people popping up undead were real. Though not in this case. She'd been autopsied already. But Mr. Harris was meticulous in his habits and so he checked again. After the wash, he positioned her hands and made sure to remove the excess gas in her body. Then I carefully turned her head to the side to give Mr. Harris better access to her carotid when her hair got tangled on my index finger. And that's when I saw it. An old scar at the base of her neck. Something that could be hidden with a t-shirt. A burn scar. The raised tissue formed three interlocking circles.

I froze.

"Jordan?" Mr. Harris said. He sounded far away. A distant planet. His eyes turned to the door to make sure it'd been left open. The Harrises knew about the closed-door thing. They made sure to leave it open. And still, I couldn't breathe. My legs started to shake. My hands still pressed against the scar.

Run. This wasn't the same voice I heard before in my head. This was a different voice.

A door I had sealed inside my headspace creaked opened. A cold room unfolded beyond. Cement floors, brick walls, the smell of dirt after rain and cages. Dog cages only they didn't hold dogs. *Do as they say, Basil. If you try to warn them, they'll kill them anyway. At least this way, they have a chance. Don't let them put you behind the door too. No one survives what's behind the door.*

I couldn't run. I couldn't even feel my legs. I pulled my thoughts into a single point inside my head. The world rippled like a placid lake disturbed by a skipping stone. I floated, nonexistent. No sound, no sight.

Whimpers tore through the darkness.

It took me a second to realize they were coming from me and that I was no longer in the prep room but sitting on something soft.

A cool sensation beginning at the back of my neck, spread throughout my body down to my toes. An angelic voice lifted me out of the darkness with a soothing sound about the Lord. I blinked my dry eyes, realizing they had been open. Unseeing. And then I sucked in a shuddering breath and collapsed into strong arms.

"There you are, sweetie," Mrs. Harris said in the darkness, overpowering everything else.

"T-trash can," I warned, right before I spewed my dinner.

Mr. Harris held me upright while Mrs. Harris held the garbage close for me to spew into it. A deluge of tears slipped down my face.

"I-I'm so-so sorry," I squeaked.

"None needed, son," Mr. Harris said. "I should've known better."

He blamed himself for my reaction to the dead body. It hadn't been the body that had made me freak out. It had been the scar on her neck. The three interlocking circles. Borromean rings. It meant Unity. Family. I should know. I had the exact same one branded at the back of my neck too.

Chapter Ten

Circles.

I'd drawn those same circles hundreds of times not knowing what I'd been drawing. They filled pages and pages inside my notebooks. Drawing them had been instinctual. It had felt right when everything around me had felt wrong.

What would Chase do if he found out he had a scar like the one on a murdered girl? Freak out. Totally, freakin' freak out. Just the way I was freaking out right now. I couldn't sleep, eat, or move. Mrs. Harris had agreed not to call Vicky regarding the episode because she did think it had been Mr. Harris's fault and they could get in trouble, and I didn't want them to get in trouble. But she asked me to call her when I got home. To take it easy for a few days. And to call her if I wanted to talk about what happened.

I agreed to all of it. I called her when I got home. And lied and told her I was okay.

I stripped myself and tried to get a better view of the scar at my neck. Vicky had told me that it had been a birthmark. But she hadn't been with me long enough to actually know what it was. My hair covered it. I'd never given it another thought. I managed to clip my hair out of the way and take a picture of it with my phone.

There it was.

Borromean rings.

My scar was smoother, as if I'd had it longer than Natalia's or as if I'd healed better.

Natalia Montenegro. I didn't even know who she was. How was it possible for two complete strangers to have the exact same scar on the exact same spot?

I searched my thoughts for answers. It wasn't a birthmark. Strike that out. It looked too identical to Natalia's to be something coincidental. The panic attack had slammed into me fast, despite the door being open. I remembered a place I'd never seen before, but unlike a two-dimensional photo of my imagination, it felt real. I'd felt the moldy air against my skin, digging in with the stench until I was saturated with it. I heard the others crying. I wanted them to stop, afraid that they'd be forced beyond the door.

Not real.

It couldn't be real.

I clutched the sink hard and closed my eyes and breathed. "Push everything away and stay focused on the present, Jordan. There is no evil behind the door. There is no cellar with cages. There are no others."

But there is you and Natalia with the same scar.

And your notebook.

Natalia Montenegro's funeral was on a Monday, and it was a school holiday, so I worked it. I made sure the family had their necessary documents signed. No one fainted. Water and bread available. The coffin was wiped down to a glossy sheen and gloves were given to the pallbearers including me and Mr. Harris.

Mrs. Harris gave me a side hug at the back of the parlor. "You touched it up beautifully."

I felt the familiar blush. I hadn't blushed so much in my sixteen years as much as I blushed working for the Harrises. It must've been a side effect of being off meds. "Her mother loved the dolphins. One of Natalia's favorite mammals." Mrs. Harris kissed my temple, though I had to lean down to receive it. "You're a good boy, Jordan." She tapped my shoulder and slipped back into the office.

Shame was an easier emotion to feel. I'd looked up Natalia on social media hoping to find something to establish the reason for our shared scars. She'd taken a trip to Mexico where she swam with live dolphins. She had looked so happy. I had to purchase some at the dollar mart. They weren't that expensive. I wasn't a good person.

Special Agent Martinez attended. He knew the family. Natalia's mom hugged him tight as she sobbed into his shoulder. Mr. Montenegro beside them. Then we drove past her home in town and headed to the burial grounds. I'd participated in over a dozen burial's while working with the Harrises. Natalia was the first murder victim.

The day was warm for early October, the ground was wet from the rains. The hole already dug, we carried the coffin to the winch where it hovered, waiting. I almost slipped inside the hole, but Special Agent Martinez caught my arm. "Be careful. The ground is unstable."

I knew that. Of course I did. My heart clamped into my throat thinking about falling in the hole and being buried alive. I nodded and walked away from the group, watching from a safe distance but unable to look away from the hole. The space between the coffin and the dirt wall didn't exceed six inches, and shadows moved around it as if trying to slip out around the light. My stomach tightened as the dark shapes solidified into pale, mud caked hands. Small hands. The hands pushed between the narrow space, digging into the wall, clawing, trying to escape. Then a shriek cut into my brain. I stumbled. My body fell inside itself again and I was looking at careful brown eyes. Special Agent Martinez had my arm and led me back away from the coffin. The coffin I'd been walking toward. I hadn't even realized I'd moved. I glanced into the hole. No shadow. No hands. No shrieks. Just a hallucination. Not real.

"Are you okay?" he asked, concern in his voice.

I rubbed the space between my brows. "I haven't eaten. I think my sugar must be crashing."

"Come on. I might have something."

I followed him to a dark blue sedan. The man moved with purpose. The bulge of his weapon visible at his waist. His dark hair curled at the edges. He had a clean face, chiseled, and his body frame suggested he liked the gym. Opposite of me. We stopped and he reached into his glove compartment and pulled out a water bottle and a granola bar.

"Breakfast of convenience," he said with a smile that felt familiar. I had words stuck in my throat. Words I should say to that but couldn't quite remember them. Like trying to catch dust motes, it faded. "Cramp?" he asked.

I realized I was rubbing the back of my neck. At the scar. Would keeping the secret I shared with the dead girl be illegal? Was I impeding a murder investigation? Letting a murderer get away? "Yeah," I said, feeling itchy. "Do you think whoever killed her is still around?" I tore the wrapper with my teeth and took a bite. It tasted like cardboard flaked with salt and sugar. I drank some of the water, feeling better. "I watch enough crime television to know that when the FBI is involved it's a big deal. And you don't look like small-town FBI either."

He chuckled, forming crinkles at the edge of his eyes. I wasn't the best judge of character, but I liked Special Agent Martinez. For a cop. "New York," he said.

I rocked on the balls of my feet. "Ah, the big cheese."

"Big Apple."

"That too."

The smile remained and I felt better seeing it. Then it fell flat as weeping brought us back to the present. "I'm sorry for your loss. Did you know her well?"

"No, but our paths did cross a very long time ago." His eyes dragged to mine like some unspoken truth lay between us. I just couldn't figure it out. "How do you do it? Doing this?" He gestured to the tombstones.

"Death? Vicky says when God was handing out empathy, I missed the class."

He laughed. "That's one way to put it, I guess."

I scratched my nose. The itchiness returned. A strange compulsion to explain myself had my thoughts rattling. "I stopped my medicine so I could have an erection. I asked your opinion about the condoms at Wally's Mart, remember?"

Special Agent Martinez pressed his lips together, but I could tell by the slight lift at the corner of his mouth that he wanted to smile. Not laugh at me like Chase, but smile. "Right, that's where I've seen you before."

"Anyways," I went on when I probably shouldn't have. "I feel a lot better though sometimes I feel sick. Like, what just happened."

"What just happened?" he asked. I didn't feel as if he were being disingenuous. Just curious.

"I thought I saw something under the casket. Maybe a cat or something." I scratched my nose again. *Liar*.

"May I ask you a question?"

"You just did."

He shook his head. "Did you know Natalia?"

"No."

"What about Liam Grant? Do you know him?"

"Not really. I mean, we go to the same school. I know of him. But he hangs around with a different crowd, you know?"

"What crowd is that?"

"The popular crowd. Is he a suspect?"

"Everyone's a suspect."

"So you think the murderer is still in town?"

"Yeah, kid. I think that's a good possibility. Be careful and report anything you might see or hear."

He handed me his business card. A very official looking one. Special Agent Nate Martinez. "Thanks," I said.

He nodded and walked back to the mourning family. Afterward, I caught Mr. Harris waiting for me near the Hearst and I headed toward him.

We slipped silently into the car, and he started to drive. "Everything okay, son?" he asked.

"Yeah, why?"

"You looked as if you've seen a ghost. I thought you were going to throw yourself at the casket. Do you want to talk about it?"

"I'm just tired." *Liar. You knew this was a possibility when you stopped taking your medication, all so that you could get laid. You are broken.* "I'm not broken," I snapped.

"Excuse me?"

Mr. Harris kept his eyes on the road because he was a safe driver, but I knew he wanted to pull over and shove my crazy out of the car. I wiped my forehead again. I hated lying.

"I…I might be feeling sick."

"Well, Mrs. Harris will fix you right up."

We reached his house and as soon as I walked inside it smelled of all things food. Not ramen or spaghettis, but real homemade food. I loved Vicky, but she was not a good cook. Breakfast was her specialty. She'd cook breakfast for birthdays and special celebrations.

Mrs. Harris kissed Mr. Harris gently on the lips.

"Go get cleaned up. Dinner's almost ready."

"Do you have some room for our boy here? He's not feeling well."

She instantly jumped to action and put the back of her hand on my forehead. "You are a sweaty mess. Come, let me take your temperature." She did. Thankfully, I didn't have a fever, or she would've called Vicky.

Mr. Harris washed up and changed into comfortable clothes. I took off my tie and jacket and washed my hands and face. Mrs. Harris refused my help to set the table. Having nothing to do, I walked around her living room, looking at all the family photos they had. The Harrises had a large family of brothers and sisters who seemed to have tons of kids, who then had kids. Generations of them. Happy smiles captured in time. Most of them missing the little boy who had his own space of photos, their son Matthew. There was a baby hospital picture of the dark-haired, dark-skinned boy with large hazel eyes. A few more baby pictures with Mr. Harris too. Then his first school picture when he'd been six. He wore a soccer team shirt, his eyes wide, happy. After that picture, there weren't any more of him. The Harrises never talked about him, at least not to me. And after that first time, I hadn't asked.

"Dinner's ready," Mrs. Harris announced.

Mr. and Mrs. Harris held hands, closed their eyes, and gave a quick prayer thanking God for the wonderful food, family, and friends, and she winked at me.

Then we started to eat.

I barely remembered my biological mother, only that she had dark hair and smelled of vanilla lip gloss. And she had no family. Vicky told me when I'd been placed into foster care that they had tried to look for family members but found nothing. After living in a group home, they decided I was too much of a needy child to remain there. I had mental problems. I had developmental delays. Too small. Too scared. Too slow. They placed me with Vicky because she had experience dealing with special needs kids. I'd been doing good.

Until you wanted to get laid.

Part of normalcy, but I wasn't normal. I thought about Jaylene cutting me off. I thought about Chase hiding our friendship, or whatever. As if I weren't good enough. I thought of Mrs. Tubbs and the critters she left me to bury. Why couldn't I just walk away without burying them?

And I thought about Natalia and the scar.

I felt as if I were looking at a movie screen of my life. I wanted to feel something, but I didn't know what I wanted to feel.

"I'm not normal," I blurted. The conversation stopped. "Something happened to me when I was a kid and now I can't feel things like normal people do. I'm not normal."

Mrs. Harris didn't reach out to comfort me or like Vicky, tell me I was perfect the way God made me.

"Well, do you like the food?" Mrs. Harris asked.

"Yes, ma'am."

"And do you like working for Mr. Harris and me?"

"Yes, I do." A touch of panic made my voice higher. Were they going to fire me?

"Well, that's good enough for me. We can start with those feelings and figure the rest out as we go."

"Really?" There must've been shock on my face because Mrs. Harris smiled.

"Honey, everyone is a touch different. It's what makes us all unique."

I was blushing. Again.

"There's nothing wrong with being different, Jordan," Mr. Harris added. "As long as you aren't hurting yourself or anyone else."

Chase had alluded to the same thing. "No, sir. I wouldn't hurt anyone, and I don't take pleasure in pain."

He laughed and tapped my shoulder. "I hear you, son."

"I should go. It's late. Thank you for dinner. Do you need help cleaning up?"

"No, Jordan. Thank you for everything you do for us."

I nodded and left before I blushed again.

ELIZABETH ARROYO

Chapter Eleven

I avoided bathrooms. I avoided Aimee and Riley. I avoided Chase. And I avoided Penny, though not well enough. She sprung on me like a weed at my locker. She looked like a Penny Cartwright. Red hair, fringes, blue eyes and freckles along the bridge of her nose. She also had a big smile on her face.

"Wanna walk to lunch together?"

"No. Not really."

I'd said the wrong thing. Penny looked as if she wanted to cry. I hadn't wanted to make her cry, but I didn't want to go to lunch with her. I was going to go to the library to use the computers to investigate a dead girl. I couldn't tell Penny that. What would Chase say? He wouldn't be rude. Yes, he would.

I felt like a deer caught in headlights.

Then Jaylene walked past with Finn. This time she *did* look at me. No, she sneered at Penny. Something so obviously distasteful, as if she sucked a lemon. She left Finn walking a few paces alone before he realized she'd pulled out of his hand and headed toward me.

Poor Penny didn't see Jaylene until she was already at her back. This made me defensive of Penny, so I pulled her behind me and met Jaylene's wrath. Penny made an *oof* sound and pressed herself against my back. It made me feel good being the protector for once.

"Can I help you?" I said, because I was still an idiot.

By that time, Finn had stopped with everyone else in the hallway. They'd been waiting for this confrontation since she dumped me. Shit. She didn't dump me. This whole thing was so confusing.

Jaylene poked me in my chest. "You are going to regret this," she hissed. "All of you."

Usually, a threat by a girl because she was heartbroken would mean nothing. But Jaylene's threat sent shivers coursing through me. It wasn't what she said, but how she said it. And the look of venom in her eyes. Something darker than usual. I've known her mannerism and looks, and this look she restrained for everyone but her brother, right before she'd get violent with him because Chase was the only one who could ever get her over the edge of sanity, and I always pulled her back from it. I'd seen her try to claw his eyes out. I'd seen the scratches on his arms. The reason he always wore long sleeves, even in summer. To hide the scars. He'd lied once to the counselor. He said he'd taken to cutting himself and was sent to therapy. His parents never spoke about it. They never paid any real attention to him unless he messed up.

But Jaylene's words weren't directed at me. They were for Penny.

Then Jaylene hoofed it away from us, like a hurricane in the wind.

Penny took that opportunity to join our hands. Despite me trying to shake her loose, she held on strong. "Lunch, then?" she said with that smile.

Apparently, I'd read Jaylene all wrong because Penny hadn't even flinched from the threat.

We walked to the lunchroom holding hands.

My mission to be normal had a hiccup with the body of Natalia Montenegro having my scar, but I could forget that for a little while and be normal at school. I just needed to fake it.

Fake it.

Be someone I wasn't.

Be Chase Cooper.

I'd observed Chase enough to know his movements. Creepy, stalking aside, I wrapped my arm around Penny, loosening the tension in my body at the same time as if I didn't have a care in the world. She squealed at someone, Aimee, as it were, and we started that way. Aimee looked at me suspiciously. Riley's eyes bulged out of his eyes. Me with a GF. Actually, she wasn't my GF. I wasn't sure what she was.

Thankfully, Aimee took her out of my arm, and they started talking about homecoming. I wanted to die. Riley rolled his eyes. He wanted to die too.

I couldn't bring up my scar at the table. Although, I had wanted to brainstorm possible scenarios that could explain the scar that didn't include me being in some sort of psycho serial killer list of murder victims. As the girls huddled, I almost huddled with Riley until he sat up straight and said, "What's up?" To someone behind me.

"What's up?" Chase said and slid into the seat next to me. Our knees brushed under the table. I wasn't sure why I noticed that. Chase turned to the girls. "Hello, ladies," he said in his cool voice.

They both blushed and giggled. Riley's eyes practically lifted inside his skull.

"Brooks," Chase said. "Can we talk?"

"Uh, sure," I didn't move as he stood up. Okay, why was he leaving if he wanted to talk? I looked over at Riley whose eyes had turned wider, and he gave me that look that said, *idiot. Private talk.*

Right.

I got up and followed Chase out of the lunchroom. He walked a few paces ahead of me, so it really didn't look like we were together, together. Not that we were together or anything, but yeah.

He turned a sharp corner behind a series of lockers and stopped. "What you said, about me helping you be normal."

I felt heat rise from my neck to pepper my cheeks.

"Can we talk later?" He tensed at the scatter of noises on the other side of the lockers.

"Yeah, sure."

"I'll text you." He walked away.

My phone buzzed as I reached the lunch table.

Chase: **Meet me at the stream near Mulcahy's after school.**

Not creepy at all. Riley gave me a *What's up* look. Better than the convo with the girls and dresses. "He needs help in math." I felt itchy.

You suck at math, Riley's face said.

I ignored it.

After school, I met Chase as instructed, making sure to look out for booby traps. The stream was technically out of Mrs. Mulcahy's property, but I didn't trust the scorn of someone who hated me. Mrs. Tubbs made an appearance at the edge of the property, watching me with her cat eyes, warning me to step closer. I almost did just to see if she'd left me a kill but then I caught sight of Chase and I didn't care enough about the bait. He stood at the edge of the stream, wearing dark jeans, boots, and his letterman's jacket. He studied something in the woods beyond the stream as he flicked a stone. It skittered three times before it sank.

I made enough noise that he turned to me as I approached. His expression was unreadable. I watched the stream and shoved my hands in my pockets, unsure what I was supposed to do or say. The moment felt peaceful. I actually didn't want to break it.

He did.

"What happened with Mrs. Mulcahy's cat? Did you really try burying it alive?"

And that ended my peace. "No," I said.

He tossed another stone. It skipped twice and sank. Every time he tossed a stone, he'd let out a heavy breath. "Why did you get in trouble then?"

"Because I was burying a dead rat."

He arched a brow.

"I may have buried fourteen critters on her property. But she only knows of three." I lifted three fingers to accentuate my point.

"Why do you do that, Jordan?"

The hairs along my arms bristled. I wanted Chase to accept me for me. I wanted him to understand me and like me. "Because dead things need to be buried. Is that why you brought me here? To accuse me of the attempted murder of a cat?"

"Well, you accused me of being a classist prick as if I cared that you're poor."

I opened my mouth and closed it. "I apologized for that. Are you always going to throw it in my face?"

"No."

I picked up a rock and threw it. It didn't skip. Just sank.

"You have to find a flat rock, and flick your hand, releasing it fast." He did it. The rock skipped three times and sank.

I started looking for a rock.

"Here, I have some." I took the rock, brushing my cold fingers against his surprisingly warm ones. He lifted his eyes to mine at the contact and I wished I could read his mind. "Just flick it, like this." He demonstrated his technique.

I followed and it skipped once. "Ha!" I felt so proud of myself. I didn't know this was a thing. It felt like a thing. "I did it!"

Chase laughed. "You're a fast learner. Try again."

We spent the rest of the afternoon skipping stones

until we drifted further upstream looking for more. Then we just started collecting some cool ones. I found the first one, excited. "It looks like bee dung," Chase said as he held it in his hand, examining it.

"It's a garnet. I can smooth it and polish it and make something."

"What would you make with it?" he asked, not believing me.

"A charm. It's a good size to hang off a leather cord or something."

He handed it to me. "Then make it for me."

I swallowed the lump in my throat as I carefully took the rock. It meant more to me now. "Yeah, sure. I can do that." I shoved it into my pocket.

Before I knew it, it'd gotten dark. Our shoes were wet, and it was getting cold. "We should probably head back."

He followed me to my house. "You can come inside if you want. I'll make some hot chocolate," I said before I considered if that was a thing guys did. I realized I didn't feel as if I had to care around Chase. I could be myself.

I tossed my bag on the sofa near my notebook and headed to the kitchen to heat up the milk.

"Where's Vicky?" he asked, closing the door behind him.

"She's working nights and sometimes stays the day with Jack."

"Ew," he said. "Sorry, I know she's your foster mom."

"I know."

I watched as Chase glanced at everything in my house. There wasn't much. A brown plaid sofa in the living room facing a small television set on a brown bookcase. My bedroom was the only room to the left of the kitchen, divided by a thick navy-blue drape. The other end of the hallway led to the bathroom, Vicky's room, and an extra bedroom. The two windows in the front room let some light in, but not enough to say it was bright and cheery. It was more shaded and sadder. As if Vicky were hiding us. You wouldn't think that a beautiful sprawling community lurked close with houses belonging to Liam and Chase. I poured the chocolate into two mugs and waited for the milk to heat up while Chase slowly perused the room. Vicky lived a Spartan life. That's what she called it. She had minimal pictures of her own family and a few of me.

The milk heated and I added it to the mugs and carried them over to the coffee table.

"Thanks," he said.

I really liked him thanking me. I liked him in my house. I liked him looking at my things and at my life. Jaylene had never wanted to come inside. She said it was too claustrophobic. He took a sip of the chocolate and smiled. Chase liked chocolate. He plopped down on the sofa and put the mug on the table in front of him. "So, not to be mean, but being alone here would creep me out. Now I know why you spent so much time at my house."

I sat down beside him. There was only one sofa. I had no choice. The small space between us felt smaller. "That's not the reason I spent so much time at your house. I just liked being there."

"With Jay."

I didn't say anything.

He rubbed his hands together, nervously. "Those drawings. They were pretty detailed. I didn't think my birthmark was so noticeable."

Shit. Shit. Shit. My breath got stuck in my throat. He didn't look at me while I finally let out the breath I'd been holding. "I'm sorry." He stood up and I stood up, panicked. I did something wrong. I was bad. And I had to be punished. The thought flittered into my mind so fast, I flinched from the intrusion. "No one knows it's you. I swear."

"Why?"

"Because I wouldn't tell anyone."

A hint of a blush peppered his cheeks. "Why did you draw me, Jordan? Why *that*?"

Oh, right. "I don't know. I just. It was beautiful. You were beautiful and it stayed in my head. I needed to draw it to put it somewhere else." It hadn't been until he flushed that I realized the words I'd just spewed. I called him beautiful.

"Why would *I* stay in your head?"

"I don't—"

He didn't let me finish. "I saw Liam in your car," he said before I could spew some more words. "He hurts people he dates. I don't want to see you hurt."

"I'm not dating him." Why would I? I didn't like Liam like that. Did I? Could I? Thoughts I'd never contemplated rushed through my mind. Did I like boys? And why would Chase say that like he hadn't cared that I like boys.

"I can help you be normal, if you still want it." Chase pulled me back into the present and out of my mind. He wanted to help me. I wanted him to help me.

"Yeah. I still want it."

He looked like he wanted to say more, but he didn't. He walked to the door, and I wanted to tell him not to go. He turned around. "Thanks for the chocolate. Maybe we can look for stones again."

"Yeah, while you explain to me all the intricacies of being normal." I snorted like an idiot.

He smiled and it was radiant.

So radiant that I thought of that smile even after

he was long gone, and I fell asleep.

ELIZABETH ARROYO

Chapter Twelve

Back in the cellar I was a tiny thing watching under shadows, in corners, never seen. "They shouldn't cry," the boy said. "The Parent will be upset."

"Then help them stop crying. You know the Parents better than we do. Help us survive."

The heavy beats of footsteps pounded just outside the door. They were coming. He was coming. My heart raced and I clutched onto Teddy until I couldn't feel my fingers.

The door swung open and there he stood.

Chase.

A silent scream forced my mouth open. Nothing came out because I'd shoved my fist in my mouth and proceeded to bite it until I tasted blood. I let out a gasp, my eyes clearing. The room coming to focus. *My* bedroom.

Everything else had been a nightmare.

Rain pelted the roof. A tap, tap, tap that felt like ghosts knocking to get inside. My brain hurt just behind my eyes. A pulsing that wouldn't stop. I'd never dreamt before, or if I had, I never remembered it. But I remembered this one. The cellar. The cages. The stink. And the Parents. It's what we called them. *The Parents*, because they weren't *our* parents.

Once the dream faded, I washed the blood from my knuckles in the bathroom transfixed by the bright red against the ceramic white as it swirled down the drain. An empty void where no one would find them.

The bodies belonging to the screams.

I knocked on my temple with a closed fist. "Get out. Get out." I needed to get this out of my head. I wanted my own fuzzy brain back. I needed to feel like me again. *Me. Me. Me.*

"What would Chase do?" I whispered.

He'd do whatever it took to feel better.

Whatever. It. Took.

Ignoring the cold, beating, rain, I snuck out of my house. I made a pit stop at the tool shed and picked up my small shovel, pick, and a flashlight. Not that the flashlight would do much good under the deluge.

I walked past Mrs. Mulcahy's property.

I just had to find the dead thing. *Dead things can't hurt you.*

And it had to be already dead. Vicky had made sure to drill that into my brain after I had almost buried Tommy William's stray cat. They didn't let us have animals at the shelter, but Tommy fed this scrawny thing and even named it Mister. Just Mister. I had found Mister wet and still on the side of the dirt path. I thought it was dead. I started to bury it when Tommy had caught me. He punched me in the face and took off with Mister. Mister hadn't been dead. Just hurt. They blamed me for that too. "Jordan," Vicky had said with such kindness in her eyes. "Killing anything alive is wrong."

"What about ants?" I had asked.

"Insects are okay. But anything else, you should ask first. Okay?"

Two days later, Vicky had officially become my foster mom and she'd taken me to see Dr. Cooper. Dr. Colleen Cooper had asked me some questions and talked to Vicky about what to do with me as I wondered about how her fish could breathe inside the water tank. She finally told me I could bury dead things, but I had to make sure they were dead.

Easy.

Dead things didn't have a heartbeat.

Dead things didn't breathe.

Dead things didn't move when you poked them.

I broke out into the road bordering the property. It didn't take long to find a vole lying on its side. It looked like it'd been hit by a car. I dropped on my knees beside its small body. The rain diluted the blood and the dark masked everything else.

Carrion served a purpose. They fed scavengers like vultures. After they had their feast, the left behind were then infested with flies and their eggs. A feast for the dermestid beetles. The cycle was an important part of the ecosystem. Nothing gets wasted. And yet, I couldn't just leave it there. Exposed.

The rain didn't let up. My clothes and hair were drenched, and I was cold. There was no way to save it. Sometimes they died. The boy had told me that. The boy with the voice in my head.

"It'll be okay," I whispered. It's what people always said when things weren't okay.

Death seemed such a simple thing. Peaceful and normal. At least without the screams.

I waited until I was sure it was dead before I buried it.

I didn't remember the walk back home, or slipping into my bed, but I'd managed both and woke up caked in mud. No more dreams. I hid under the covers until Vicky left the house and then shoved the sheets into the laundry before showering.

Getting the mud out from under my fingernails required more effort than my aching muscles cared for and the scratches on my hands stung along with the teeth marks on my knuckles. I wrapped as much of it as I could in bandages and then called Aimee, who was stuck in Catechism this rainy Saturday morning. To Riley's house I went. Lying on his bed, he tossed a ball into the air. It tapped the ceiling before coming down into his hand like a heartbeat.

I sat at his desk using his computer. I didn't have one at home, and cell phones were a pain to use when I didn't know what I was searching for. And except for Natalia's Montenegro's basic information, I had nothing else.

"Why are you looking into Natalia again?"

Because we share the same scar and that has to mean something. "I'm just curious. Aren't you?"

Tap.

"Nope, she's dead."

Tap.

"Yeah, I figured that out when I helped Mr. Harris embalm her and put her in a hole."

Tap.

"You're gross, dude."

I rolled my eyes.

I would've preferred having this conversation with Aimee, who studied personality traits in her psychology class and could give me a clue as to what I should be looking for in a murderer.

"So, you and Penny, huh?" Riley started.

"There is no me and Penny."

"But you're taking her to homecoming, right?"

I typed into the search engine and more information came up about Natalia Montenegro's death, but nothing about the scar. Natalia seemed well loved in her UM community. Involved in lots of activities.

The tapping stopped.

"Woah, go back." Riley said, startling me into pausing at the picture of Natalia posing for a photo with a group of students last summer. "That's Jaylene Cooper."

I leaned in closer and didn't see anyone that looked like Jaylene Cooper. "Where?"

"Right there," he pointed at the screen.

The image of that person was clearly female, but the picture cut her head. "How could you tell?"

"I know those boobs in that t-shirt anywhere."

I turned back to the picture. I didn't recognize the t-shirt in question, or the boobs and thought Riley had lost his mind. But I did recognize the thin silver chain around her neck and the feldspar pendant I had made for her.

Jaylene had known Natalia. Why did I suddenly feel creeped out that Jaylene knew Natalia?

I shut the computer down. "Thanks."

"Hey, are you going to tell me what's going on?"

"Nope. But I'll talk to you in school."

I didn't talk to him in school but avoided him and Aimee instead. I'd dug into Natalia some more and didn't find anything that would link her to me.

Except Jaylene.

But that was pretty far-fetched. Unless Jaylene had a similar scar as mine.

ELIZABETH ARROYO

Chapter Thirteen

Halloween made the town come alive. Town square had been transformed into a spooky ghost town complete with build your own cemetery kits for half off when you add a special slaughterhouse to the purchase. Blood sold by the gallon, half priced, and of course haunted ranches galore. One such ranch featured a scary hayride through a corn maze filled with the freaky.

On Vicky's day off, we spent the evening walking Main Street together. It felt nice to just be with her, especially after lying to her for so long. It'd been a week since the burial, and I hadn't had any more hallucinations. And I kept thinking about what Aimee said about me making decisions for myself. I didn't want to lie about not taking the medication anymore. I hated lies.

"Vicky?" I said.

"Jordan?" she said.

"Can we talk about my medications?"

I felt her stiffen a little bit beside me. "Sure. What's up?"

"What if I don't want to take them anymore?" I didn't dare look at her while I said the next thing. "Aimee is majoring in psychology and says I can have patient autonomy now and choose my course of treatment." True. Not a lie. She also used me as her research topic, promising me anonymity. I kept thinking about what Chase said about her being my friend *and* a psych major. Was that on purpose? Or coincidence? Did she just want to study me?

"Jordan? What do you want to do?"

Right. My question. I seemed to live in my head

sometimes. I bit my bottom lip, dragging a layer of skin. "I want to stop taking the medications."

She sighed. "Are you sure? We only want what's best for you."

"We?"

She sighed. "Me and Dr. Cooper."

I didn't think I wanted to get back on those medications. Although my brain malfunctioned without them. "I'm sure."

She stopped to face me. "Just promise me, no lies. Okay? If we do this, and you start experiencing things you shouldn't, you'll be honest with me."

An itch on my lower back made me shift on my feet. "I will."

"I'll reach out to Dr. Cooper and schedule an appointment. Good enough?"

I nodded. *Liar.* I already started this lie. I'd have to see it through.

We started walking again. "In the meantime…" Vicky plucked a flyer announcing a spooky corn maze equipped with all the lathering of someone trying to rip another's face off. "You should go with your friends. It'll be fun."

"I don't think imagining someone trying to kill me would be fun."

She pressed her lips together trying not to laugh. "You might be the only one."

I'd have to remember to ask Chase if imagining someone trying to kill me would be fun. Chase had been teaching me how to be normal during our rock excavations near the stream. I'd shaped and glossed the garnet and gave it to him on a leather strap. He'd taken it like a badge of honor, making me feel…tingling.

We were in his backyard shooting hoops. I knew he was hiding our whatever-this-was, but I didn't care.

He'd still say hi to me in the hallways at school, made it a point to choose me in gym whenever he could, and when he couldn't he'd block me whispering what I needed to do to make a point, and we'd text each other.

I wore a hoodie, while Chase wore a thermal under a t-shirt with Monkey Swine heat-sealed on it. I hadn't gotten the nerve to ask him about the story behind that name. I dribbled the basketball in front of him after telling him about the corn maze thing.

"You should go. Take Penny," he said. Then he stole the basketball and dunked it, his body moving in total perfection. He grabbed the basketball and came back to center with a smile.

"Show off."

He laughed. "Again." He tossed me the ball. I caught it with a grunt.

This time, I used my ass to keep him away. He loomed over me, and his hand landed on my hip. That did not help with my concentration. Too close. I leaned in with my shoulder, twisted my hips to throw the ball. It flew two inches before he slammed it down.

"You are freakishly tall. You know that?" I admonished as he ran for the ball and brought it back. His cheeks rosy from the cool air.

"You have to be more aggressive. Don't be afraid of body contact."

Yeah, he knew me well.

"Fine," I said surer than I felt.

I dribbled, ass to his front, and ignored his looming body. Making note of the position of his feet, I faked left, went right, and slammed my face into his elbow. The ball ripped out of my hands, and I started to fall, bracing myself for a wounded pride. Instead, he tried to save me, our feet got tangled and we fell together. He landed on top of me, bracing my head with his hand so I wouldn't crack my skull on his cement driveway. We both let out a whoosh of breath as we made impact with the ground.

His body stretched out over mine, from chest to feet. Then, I spread my legs and he sank down against me. There. He sagged down *there*. And he lowered his eyes to my lips. It sent a sensory overload throughout my body and my cock jerked behind my pants. He felt it. I knew he felt it because his breathing deepened, and a strange expression crossed his features. Something changed between us in that moment. I didn't think he even knew what it was.

Instinctively, he rutted against me. For a fraction of a second, I felt the bulging in his pants too. The hardness against mine. And it felt better than anything I'd ever felt before. But he must've done it by accident, because he jerked up as if the touch burned him. It burned me too, but not in the same way.

The laugh turned awkward. "Are you okay?"

No, I wasn't. I felt dizzy. I took his hand and he helped me to my feet. That's when I noticed the blood. "You're bleeding."

He looked at the cut as if it was nothing. But he got it for saving me. "It's nothing."

"We should clean it up."

He reached behind his head and pulled off his black t-shirt, bunching it in his hand so he wouldn't trail blood inside the house. That's when I noticed the garnet around his neck. It made me feel even more loopier. I followed him to his bathroom. He and Jaylene had their own bathrooms. I'd been in his room before but now it felt awkward. Different. As if I were seeing it for the first time. The awkward moment stretched on as I cleaned his cut and wrapped it.

"Maybe you need to see a doctor. Get stitches.

There's so much blood."

"I don't need stitches. And I didn't know you were squeamish. I thought you worked at a mortician's place."

"Funeral home. Yeah."

"So blood is worse than dead bodies?"

"Yeah. You shouldn't have saved my head."

"Well, don't tell anyone."

"I won't. Your secret is safe with me."

He pulled his hand back and scowled at me. "What secret?"

"Me. Us. Being friends." I could've sworn he flinched, but he turned away too quickly for me to be sure.

"Yeah, you should go before Jay gets home."

Okay, that shouldn't have hurt as much. I should be used to Chase cutting me off. Whenever anyone caught us talking, he'd just say see you later and walk off, even if we were in the middle of a conversation. And he was always jittery when we were in public. The only thing I'd learned about being normal from him is how to hide not being normal.

"Yeah," I said. "Okay."

I walked to the door, maybe hoping he'd walk me out. He didn't. He walked into his bathroom and closed the door.

I stopped in the hallway just to compose myself. I shouldn't care so much. Hell, I didn't care much about Riley whenever he left me to be with someone else. It didn't hurt like *this*. I would've thought more about it, but Jaylene's opened bedroom door caught my attention. The door didn't pulse, no screams wafted from behind it. Just a normal door. In a normal house. Leading to a room I'd spent countless hours inside.

No biggie.

A strange sensation of anticipation gutted me. Then I pushed the door open the rest of the way, letting it move on its own, and stepped inside. Where once was order, stood destruction. Jaylene's room had been torn apart. Clothes, makeup, and ripped pages littered the floor. Her mattress was bare, the mirror above her dresser cracked. Posters were poked with holes. Eyes, mouths, throats slit. Her room was one loud scream.

"What the hell?" Chase shoved me out of her room and slammed the door closed.

I couldn't unsee what I'd seen.

Chase sighed and ran his hand through his hair. He'd changed to a short sleeve t-shirt. Claw marks lined his forearm, from elbow to wrist. Red and angry. At that moment, I knew that Vicky had been wrong about me. I didn't suffer from lack of feelings. I didn't lack empathy, nor the ability to tell right from wrong, because what happened to Chase was *wrong*. With him, I felt things I'd never felt before. The numbing gone, replaced by a scatter of emotions I had no name for. "Did I do that?" I pointed to the room. "Is that because of me?"

"Does it matter? You should leave."

I should. But I couldn't move. "Just because she's sick doesn't mean it's okay for her to hurt you."

For a moment, I saw the tears in his eyes. His lip trembled slightly. About to break my fear of being rejected by him and hug him, I heard the front door opening and it shattered the moment. Panicked, he shoved me into his room and locked me inside.

"Where is he?" I heard Jaylene's angry voice on the other side of the door just before the world shifted.

The door. Chase stood behind the door. Panic started to flare up inside of me, burning a path of poison through my veins.

"I know he's here. His piece of shit car is outside.

What are you doing with him?" Jaylene's muffled words grounded me.

I couldn't hear Chase's response, but I did hear the crack of a slap. "You better not get in my way," she said, and stormed off. I heard her door slam.

Please. Open the door. Open the door.

I realized I was pressed against his dresser, my eyes glued to the door.

Time slowed with no reference when the door finally opened. I couldn't move as our eyes locked on each other. I saw the small pity in his eyes before his expression slipped into a tight mask. The red welt on his cheek almost made me sob.

"Chase," I couldn't even finish my thought. My voice broke. I wanted to hug him. To protect him from all the evil in the world. But I couldn't even save him from beyond the door.

"Are you okay?" he asked.

That he asked me instead of the other way around made my heart launch into my throat and I nodded because words were useless.

"I'll walk you out." Without waiting, he walked out of the room. I had no choice but to follow. Silently creeping past Jaylene's bedroom, I headed down the stairs to the front door already opened for me. Everything I wanted to say stuck in my throat.

ELIZABETH ARROYO

Chapter Fourteen

Chase avoided me like bad news for the remainder of the week. Maybe a normal person would've taken the hint and stayed away from him. But I couldn't. The reason I ended up at the Grant Ranch and Haunted Corn Maze. Yeah, Liam's parents hosted a haunted treat in their ten-acre property.

"You should pay more attention to her," Aimee said, watching Riley and Penny laughing at one of the scarecrows that hung askew as we waited for the horse and carriage to move.

They looked like they were having fun. I didn't want to interrupt by trying to pay attention to her. "I don't think she needs my attention." Aimee gave me a look I couldn't interpret. Then our attention turned to the new group getting on the carriage ride. My heart started to wallop in my chest making me equally dizzy and sick to my stomach.

Chase boarded the carriage with Tabatha glued to his side like a wart. Liam leading the entourage caught a glimpse of me and added to my torture by taking the bench seat in front of us. He had a pencil behind his ear, and he leaned back brushing his knees against mine.

Chase didn't look at me at all. Tabatha practically took position on his lap, and they started sucking faces.

I jumped out of my seat and stabbed her in the eye with Liam's pencil. With a wet sucking sound, her eye popped free of her eye socket. Blood poured down her face and she let out a blood curdling scream.

My heart started to race in my chest. My body vibrated with some unnamable force that spun me out of reality for a few seconds before I crashed into a reality so skewed, I couldn't be sure I actually landed until I heard Liam.

"Get a room, Cooper," Liam said, breaking me from my headspace.

The world shimmered in front of me, returning to normal with Chase and Tabatha still sucking faces while I watched from my seat. I hadn't stabbed her with a pencil. Her eye hadn't sprung free from her skull. I'd done nothing wrong. Then, I started to laugh. A sound so random, so loud, that I couldn't stop. Every face turned to me as tears slid down my face. I didn't even know why I was laughing, only that it felt good. Aimee looked at me as if she wanted to dissect my brain, which made me laugh harder. Penny sidled closer to Riley who didn't move away, which made me cringe inside. Then Liam kicked my toes and cocked his head as if he knew what I'd just been thinking.

Monster.

Killer.

Psycho.

I wasn't a monster or a killer. I wasn't. A psycho, maybe. I wasn't sure yet. I wiped my wet cheeks as the outburst died down, then I kicked him back just because.

"What's so funny, Brooks?" Liam asked.

I shook my head. "Everything."

They all looked at me as if waiting for my head to explode in confetti. Thankfully, the five other people that got on the carriage got their attention. Jaylene and Finn took a seat away from us. And Steel Morrison plus two dropped onto the bench seat near the exit. Between Jaylene and Steel, I wasn't sure who wanted to kill me first. And as the horse started pulling us into the woods, I realized I just gave them ample opportunity.

Chase slowly dragged his eyes my way. What did he expect me to say? Save me? I had two perfectly good feet to run and a good set of lungs to scream. I didn't need Chase.

The horses stopped at the beginning of the maze, and I suddenly did not want to get off. Aimee, Penny, and Riley got off first, then Chase and his band mates. Jaylene and Finn followed, and Steel got to his feet just as I did. I hated that he was taller than me, bigger, and mean.

"Ladies first," he said with that crooked grin he wore so well.

I started forward and just as I got to the first step, he shoved me hard. I should've braced for it. Anticipated it. I didn't. I tumbled the last few steps until I landed on hands and knees on the ground. Laughter followed.

"Oops," he said. "Watch your step, dude."

"Creep," Penny said, helping me up. No one else moved to help me.

"Grow a pair, Brooks." Tabatha chuckled.

Chase ground his teeth as if restraining the urge to punch Steel in his face. Or at least that's what I wanted to believe. Chase could very well want to punch me in the face for being pathetic.

If this was normal, I wanted no part in it. I felt the sting of tears close, and I hated them. I hated feeling. Feelings sucked.

Steel, Miller, and Trace disappeared laughing, while Tabatha coaxed Chase to leave the path too and they slipped away from the group. The other band members scattered, Liam too. And when I turned to look for my friends, they were gone too.

It was just me and corn.

I couldn't see over the corn stalks to where my friends headed off to. Though lights were spread throughout, visibility was nil and I had to use my phone's flashlight to see because, yeah, right, Aimee had the flashlight. I hated this. I hated scary. I hated Halloween. I didn't move for a full minute. I counted to sixty sure that at least Aimee would come back for me. Then the sounds started. A long howl in the distance. Chains rattled. And then screams.

They weren't real screams. I'd heard real screams before. The speakers crackled with static and backflow. Not real. I started to move where I figured my friends had headed. "Aimee!" I half-whispered, half-yelled when I saw the stalks move and it wasn't from the nonexistent wind. Laughter followed.

Steel.

The hairs on my body stood on end. He hated me for some reason. Maybe because I got him into drugs. I'm sure he'd been on something before. Or maybe it was because he was bigger than me. I was smaller. An easy target. Targets were the weak. The ones who showed their emotions. The ones who *cared*. The weak needed to be destroyed. Punished.

You're not weak, Basil, are you?

The voice cut through the silence and made me stop moving. This wasn't my normal voice that criticized my life choices. This voice belonged to a Parent.

I was back *there*. The farmhouse. The basement. Inside the cage. The Parents would come for me. They'd take me behind the door with the screams.

"No," I whispered. "I'm not weak." My rapidly beating heart suggested otherwise.

Good. Bring me one, or I'll take Kale behind the door. You don't want that, do you?

I shook my head. *No. No. No.* Behind the door was bad. Real bad.

I didn't want Kale hurt. He was my brother. We were all family. Had to protect each other. It's what our brand meant. Family. Union. Together forever and ever.

A scream blasted near me. A real scream and I ran. I darted out of the path and into the corn.

Find an adult. Do you remember Henry, the old man at the Wicker Farm? Someone like that. He'll help you. Just show him. Can you do that, Basil? This voice belonged to the boy I trusted to save us.

No. I couldn't. Tears streamed down my face. I veered left. The corn stalks moved. Hands reached for me, tugged on my hoodie. Footsteps pounded behind me, in front of me, everywhere. I couldn't see. Then the screams started. The door. *You don't want to be the one caught behind the door.*

I slammed into an immovable object hard enough to knock me on my ass. A tree. I'd slammed into a damn tree. Pain buzzed in my head. I felt the trickling of blood down my temple. I didn't want to move. The night sky full of stars.

They're beautiful, aren't they? the boy said.

I wasn't there anymore. The Parents were gone. My brothers and sisters were gone. I couldn't remember them, so they were gone. I was here. In a corn maze with my friends and my not friends. I wasn't a little kid anymore. I was sixteen. I'd survived.

It's better if he forgets.

The memory slipped away but I knew it'd been my mom talking. Not the evil owners of the door, not *The Parents,* but the ones that saved me. My biological mom. She wanted me to forget.

"Don't forget us, Basil," Sage said. "You have to make sure they come back for us. Okay?"

I couldn't forget. Not anymore. I nodded even though Sage wasn't here. Sage. They named us stupid plant names. I had been Basil, not Jordan. Kale had been my cage brother. That's what The Parents called it. Cage brother. We were responsible for each other. We could never let the other get hurt.

I wished I could close my eyes and drift off. Laughing echoed in the distance. Cat calls followed. People, life happening around me. The breeze shifted the branches above creating moving shadows like ghosts. A boy with the lightest brown eyes against the darkest skin I'd ever seen floated behind my eyes. He crouched next to me.

"Are you going to bury me?" I asked him.

"Yes, all dead things need to be buried."

I couldn't move as a heavy weight fell on my chest making it hard to breathe. Dirt covered my skin, my eyes, my mouth. I couldn't move as the dead body pressed against me.

"Wait for the rain and then run."

Thunder rumbled against the sky.

"Run, Basil, Run."

The order forced me to my feet, and I ran. The memories chased me. No matter how fast I ran, I couldn't outrun them. They pressed against the scar at my neck, forcing blurred images into my mind. A boy. A cage. The door. Always the door.

I ran.

I didn't care where I was headed. I needed to run. I needed to find someone. I didn't care who. I ran toward the sounds of voices and broke out into a clearing when I slammed into someone. The Parents. They knew. They followed me. *No. No.* I failed. They'd take me back. They'd put me behind the door where everyone screamed. Where they died. I fought. I cried out words I couldn't understand. Arms wrapped around me, and I tried to get loose. I shoved and pushed until the arms let me go and I fell on my ass again.

"Shit, Jordan. It's me."

I recognized that voice. The haze lifted and I saw

Chase standing over me. Tabatha, Liam and his crew surrounding us. "Fuck, dude, he's bleeding," Liam said.

I absently wiped the blood.

"Shit, he looks like a fucking ghost," Zac said.

"I'm too trashed to take him to the hospital. Don't tell me we have to take him to the hospital?" Ash added, on the verge of a freak-out.

Hospital? No way. "I'm fine." My voice came out shaky and I started to get up. Chase stood close as if looking to catch me should I fall, but he didn't touch me. "I'm okay."

Tabatha snorted. *Yeah, right. You're fucking insane.*

She wasn't wrong.

"I'm okay." I couldn't look at anyone. I shoved my hands in my pockets and started walking away. I made it a few steps before Chase grabbed my arm.

"It's the other way."

Right. I turned back around, my body jittery and cold. I'd lost my phone. Vicky was going to kill me. We couldn't afford another one. I stopped suddenly and Chase rammed into my back. I hadn't even known he'd been following me. "I lost my phone."

"You're not going to find it now. I'll let Liam know. Maybe his parents can have the groundskeeper look for it."

Right. "Okay." I started off again and stopped when flashlights stung my eyes and Aimee, Riley, and Penny appeared in front of me.

"What happened?" Aimee asked.

"Nothing, I'm fine. Can we go now?" My voice shook and I hated it. My whole body trembled as if I were a dry leaf in the wind. Thankfully, no one shined their light on my face. I was pretty sure I looked awful.

"We haven't reached the end point," Penny

whined.

Really? Aimee also looked at her like, *Really.*

"I'm fine," I said. "I'll just walk. It's not far." I started to walk away. I needed to move. Though my ribs hurt. My neck too. And my brain felt about ready to leak out of my ears.

"Jordan, hold up." I turned in time to hear Tabatha practically snarl, but she followed Chase. "I'll take you home."

I mumbled something unintelligible and followed the couple out of the thick corn, back to the slow grueling wagon ride back to the beginning.

The beginning. Where everything starts.

I couldn't remember my beginning. Not that I thought anyone could remember their birth. Too traumatic an event for young minds, but I couldn't remember a starting point to my chaotic mind. I tried. As I ignored Tabatha arguing with Chase, I tried to remember the face of the Parents, the face of my brothers and sisters in cages, but they were inkblots. I had to play with the idea that they probably weren't even real.

We reached the truck, and the drive was awkward. Colder inside the cab of his F150 than outside. Tabatha pouted all the way to her house because Chase dropped her off first. She climbed out and glared at him. Yeah, the *thing* led him to follow like a puppy with his tail between his legs. I wasn't sure about this sex thing, but it must be great if girls had guys doing whatever they wanted for it.

I caught them kissing, though Chase looked a little stiffer than usual. The kiss was short. Then he climbed back inside. "You can sit in the front."

"I'm good." I actually didn't want to move.

"You don't look good. Here, put this on your forehead." He handed me a small microfiber cloth. "You're bleeding. Do you need to go to the hospital?"

"No! No hospitals. I'll be fine."

He reversed out of the driveway and started for my house. No directions needed.

In the dark, the narrow dirt road leading deeper into the woods looked like a place any human with self-preservation would avoid in the dark. Vicky had gotten the house for a steal. No guessing why.

He stopped the truck in the driveway. The headlights illuminated the front which looked like the setting of a monster movie. The one where monsters hide in the basement and kill everyone. Even the lights Vicky had paved along the dirt path couldn't penetrate the dark. If anyone or anything wanted to kill me, they didn't need to chase me in the woods. They could meet me here. At home. The thought made me shiver.

Chase turned back and glared at me. "Are you sure you're okay?"

"Yeah." But I didn't move.

"Where's your mom?"

"Working."

"You're alone?" He arched a brow.

The concern in his voice after he'd been such a dick to me confused me. "Yeah."

He turned back to stare at the house for a few seconds more before he said, "Fuck it," and put the truck in reverse, turned it around, and headed back into the main road. "My hero complex expired. If anyone wants to hurt you all they have to do is wait for you to come home and beat you with kindness. You can stay with me."

I chuckled but my stomach did all sorts of weird things inside of me at the thought of staying the night with Chase.

ELIZABETH ARROYO

Chapter Fifteen

I'd slept over at the Coopers' house more times than I could count. The spare bedroom still had some of my things—clothes, books, music. The Coopers had been like family. But I'd always been with Jaylene. Staying over with Chase felt as if we were doing something wrong.

"Is Jaylene here?" I asked. The thought of what she'd do to Chase if she found out I stayed with him made me sick.

"No. She's staying with Carla." Chase parked in the driveway. "Can you walk?"

I didn't have much choice. Though my ribs hurt. "Yeah."

Although Chase acted as if it were totally normal I was sleeping over, I silently tiptoed inside. His parents' room was in the main level while all the other bedrooms were upstairs. Thankfully, our paths didn't cross. I wasn't sure what I would've told them. What excuse I'd come up with for being with Chase and not Jaylene. Chase didn't seem to care.

I followed him into his room, ignoring Jaylene's room completely this time. The door was closed. He threw his jacket on the chair and slipped into his bathroom, leaving the door slightly open. I heard the water running. I didn't know what he expected me to do, or why he brought me here, so I just stayed put. Cold settled into my bones and I hugged myself.

At that moment, I wished I could've been someone else. I wanted to forget the memories that had poured into my mind as if the walls that had been put up around them had been obliterated. I couldn't sort them out. Not the blurred faces, not the screams, and not the feeling that something was really wrong with me.

Chase walked out of the bathroom, drying his hands. His eyes landed on me. "Shit, you look like shit," he said, tossing the towel to the side among the mound of clothes he had on his floor.

"What am I doing here?"

"Do you want me to take you home?"

The thought of being alone, in that house, in the woods made me shiver. "No."

He sighed and raked his hand through his hair. "Sit down. I'm going to put butterfly stitches on that before you clean up." Chase moved closer to me and cupped my chin to look at my face.

I could hardly breathe. His eyes lowered to mine and held me suspended in an alternate reality. That's how it felt being caught in his gaze. The only person who ever really saw me. His eyes met mine, then lowered to my lips, and back up. Then he took a step back.

"I'll get the first aid kit."

He left me alone to contemplate in which reality it would be okay for Chase to like me. I wanted to live in that one.

Chase came back with the kit. With gentle, expert hands, he bandaged my forehead as I stared at the garnet on the leather cord around his neck. That he wore it and didn't toss it after pissing him off made me feel all kinds of things. His fingers pressed the wound and I winced.

"Sorry," he said. "I know it hurts."

Yeah, because he'd done this before on himself every time Jaylene hurt him. Although at times his eyes would meet mine, he kept them focused on the wounds. Biting back words with grunts every now and again. "What happened?" he finally asked. "Did Steel do this to you?"

"No," I said but didn't offer anything else.

He let out a deep sigh and got to his feet. "Get cleaned up. I'll go get you something to wear from your stash in the guest bedroom." Without a response from me, he walked out.

At least he left the bathroom door open. I walked inside and stripped out of my clothes. The mirror reflected a horrible sight. I did look like shit. My forehead wasn't the only damage. I had a scratch on my chin, a red splotch on my cheek that would probably turn purple, and my ribs hurt though I didn't think anything was broken. I started to pick at the leaves in my hair when Chase came up behind me.

I glanced at him through the mirror as his eyes slowly slid down my body. My naked body. I realized this was the first time he's ever seen me naked. I didn't shower in the boy's locker room like he did, and he'd never walked in on me while I showered in Jaylene's room or the guest bedroom.

His cheeks turned a slight shade of pink. His features hardened and then he glared at me. "The least you could do is close the door," he hissed and slammed the bathroom door shut.

The loud slam felt like a sledgehammer to my skull. I spun as soon as the door sealed me inside. My chest suddenly felt too tight. I clutched the sink at my back trying to remember how to breathe.

"You don't want to be behind the door, Basil."

Chase. Chase was behind the door.

"Basil, they're coming."

Lights danced in front of me. I couldn't breathe right. My chest hurt. I had to get Chase. I had to move. I took a step as if moving through tar when the door swung open again. A meek squeak came out of my throat. Chase stood just beyond. Alive. Not dead. No Parents. Alive.

There was something in his blue eyes that made me feel safe. And a few seconds later, he had me in his arms.

"I'm so sorry, Jordan," he whispered. "I'm sorry. I wasn't thinking. The door. I know. I'm sorry."

I wanted to melt like a puddle at his feet. I just allowed myself to breathe instead. "I just…I just don't want them to hurt you behind the door. I don't want them to hurt you."

His arms tightened around me. "No one's going to hurt me," he whispered into my ear. "I'm safe. You're safe. No one is going to hurt us."

I wanted to believe him. I did. But that jagged piece of my heart didn't let me.

After too short a time with his arms around me, he chuckled dryly. "You make me crazy." Relief touched his voice. His hands trailed the length of my spine, and I realized I was naked in his arms, and I didn't feel vulnerable or wrong. I felt good. He pulled back and made a point to keep his eyes on my face. "Take a shower. I'll wait for you in bed." He shook his head as if warding away a thought. "In my room. Whatever," he finally said and walked out. This time leaving the door open.

Open is safe.

No one ever tried clawing an open door.

I pushed that thought aside and climbed into the bathtub and showered. When I finished, I dried myself and wrapped the towel around my hips. Chase was sitting on his bed, the guitar across his lap as he played something. It sounded nice.

"I found some PJs," he lifted his chin to his desk where he'd left me a white tee and some SpongeBob PJ bottoms. I dropped the towel and my skin instantly cooled as I pulled on the pants with no underwear and put on the white tee. When I turned back to him, he was staring at me in a way that made my body tingle, everywhere.

He cleared his throat and scooted out of the bed. "You could, um, take the guest bedroom, or stay here. I don't mind." He put the guitar back and slipped into the bathroom. He left the door open.

I didn't want to go to the guest bedroom. I glanced around his room.

Chase had always been a big question mark I had found fascinating. Maybe I had come over more than I should've because I wanted to see him. Jaylene had been a side note. But he'd never wanted to be my friend, so this attention from Chase was new for me. Chase's dark walls were full of metal band posters. He had four crates full of vinyl albums, three guitars, one hung on the wall, and music stuff around the room. I sat at his desk and flipped through his notebook filled with poems and lyrics. I became instantly lost in his words of love, loss, pain and regret. Some were just angry songs.

"Nosey much?"

I jumped to my feet feeling guilty. Guilty! A new feeling for me. "Sorry."

He took the notebook from my fingers and closed it. "Don't look at my shit."

"Okay," I whispered, feeling a slight sting in my chest. "Do you want me to go?"

He passed me to go to the bed, and I caught a hint of his shampoo and soap scent. No longer wearing eyeliner and with his long hair loose and wet around his shoulders he looked vulnerable as if he'd wiped away the mask he showed everyone else and let himself be himself just for me. I got to see all his versions and Chase Cooper was the most gorgeous thing I'd ever seen in my life. "Do what you want, Jordan," he said. Not mad. Just stated it like a fact. He turned off the lights and climbed under the covers and waited.

I climbed in next to him. "This isn't weird?"

"Don't make it weird."

This was weird enough.

I laid on my side facing him. He laid on his back, his hands on his chest, staring at the ceiling. I didn't want to make it weird. I closed my eyes, listening to his breathing.

"Jordy," he whispered. "What happened tonight? You really scared me when you screamed."

I wanted to tell him everything. But that would only make me sound crazy. Even in my head, hearing voices, seeing people that weren't there, was crazy. "I just got scared. I'm okay," I lied. "Go to sleep and stop making this weird."

I waited until his breathing evened out before I could finally let myself sleep.

Chapter Sixteen

I opened my eyes and, for a moment, my surroundings felt unfamiliar. Until my brain caught up to current events. I'd freaked out at the corn maze. I stayed with Chase. On his bed. With him beside me. I remembered he hadn't been touching me when we'd fallen asleep. Now, he was curled into my back. His arm slung over my chest, one leg over my hip. I became hyperaware of every touch point. His hairy legs on mine, his arm around my waist, and the heat of his body pressed against my back.

I wasn't sure how we ended up in this position, but I didn't want to move. It made something I'd been avoiding very clear. I liked Chase more than just a friend. More than just someone I wanted to be like. I liked Chase. I liked his smile. I liked feeling his hands on me and when he protected me. I liked listening to him play his guitar. I liked Chase in ways I'd never liked anyone else. I didn't want to think about what that meant about my sexuality. I'd had enough labels to last a lifetime. I didn't want to label this. Somehow, labeling it would make it impersonal. I wanted how I felt to be about *him*.

He shifted and I felt his erection brush one of my butt cheeks. Then he did it again. Morning wood. This was something normal for teenage boys. Just hormonal. It meant nothing. Chase could be having a dream about someone else. That thought hurt too. But Chase made it very clear that we couldn't be friends out in the open. He'd only tolerate my level of crazy in private. Sure, he'd protected me in front of his friends, but that had to be out of some sense of duty. Maybe he had a hero complex or something. He would've helped anyone. It had nothing to do with me.

That thought made me want to wake him up. I didn't want to be a sex toy to be used right now to satisfy his stupid dream. He rutted against me again and I hit him with an elbow. He flinched and growled.

"Don't be such a grouch," he said, but he hadn't let me go.

"This is weird. Let me go."

"No. You're warm."

That made me blush. To get him away, I tilted my hips, hitting him with my ass. Yeah, I felt that hard prod against my ass again, and he moaned. Moaned or groaned, I couldn't tell. But he laughed. "You honestly think you can wrestle with me?"

No, but I tried anyway. Two moves later he had me pinned under him, laughing. "I should teach you how to fight, weakling."

Wanting to show him I wasn't a weakling, I wrapped my legs around his hips and twisted, forcing him on his back until I was straddling him. "What were you saying?"

He jerked his hips up, but I clung to him like a baby monkey, digging my face into the crook of his neck, pressed against his body until he finally laughed and went boneless. "Fine. You win. You monkey." He started tickling me, surprising me. I let him go and tickled him back until he fell over the bed.

"Shit. Are you okay?" If I hurt him, I'd never forgive myself. He lay sprawled on the floor clutching his stomach laughing. "You are a weirdo." *A beautiful weirdo*.

That only got him laughing harder. At least until someone knocked on his door. On instinct, I threw the covers over me, from head to toe.

"Chase," his mother said, not opening the door.

Their parents believed in privacy. "Come down to breakfast. Your father wants to talk to you."

Chase climbed onto the bed again and tore the covers away from me. I pulled the pillow on my head as if that would hide the rest of me. "Okay," Chase said laughing to his mother. He pulled the pillow away from my face. "Why are you hiding?"

I let out a frustrating sound. "Don't you think it'd be weird for them to find me here?"

He plopped on the bed beside me. "I'm allowed overnight guests."

"That's what I am? An overnight guest?"

He shrugged. Our eyes met. He was close enough that all I had to do was lean over and kiss him.

He huffed and sat up, swinging his legs over the bed. "Get dressed. We have to talk to my parents during breakfast." He grabbed some clothes and headed to the bathroom while I realized I had no clothes to change into. I put on last night's clothes and shoes and was ready when he came out looking like Chase again. Complete with liner around his eyes. They made them pop. I liked it on him.

I followed him again down the stairs. I meant to shoot for the exit, walk home, or take the bus, but he grabbed my hand. "Uh, uh."

"I don't want them to see me."

"They want to talk and you're my excuse to not talk. You owe me for saving your life."

"You didn't save my life," I hissed.

"I did. Kind of."

I stopped arguing with him since he started to drag me to the kitchen. His mother looked up from her plate at me, confusion set in and then a smile. Short and plump with a head of chestnut hair and brown eyes, Mrs. Cooper looked nothing like Jaylene or Chase. "Jordan, are you here for Jaylene?"

I could've lied, but I didn't. "No, I had an accident last night and Chase helped me."

Mr. Cooper glared at Chase over his coffee. Mrs. Cooper's smile remained.

"Yeah," Chase added. "We have to go."

"Chase," his father said. "Sit."

Chase scowled and glanced at the door, probably considering making a run for it and leaving me behind.

"You can have a seat too," Mr. Cooper said to me.

I sat down. Chase glared at me as if this were my fault. I ignored him.

"Mrs. Mills called me yesterday. Do you have any idea why?"

Chase wiped his nose and started bobbing his knee up and down in a nervous twitch. "I sideswiped her car."

"Yes, you did. This is the second infraction with that truck. You promised to be responsible."

"I'll pay for the damages."

"Yes, you will. She wants you to help her around her property. I told her you'd be there every day after school to do what she needs."

He snorted. "I'm not a fucking handyman."

"Language," his mother scolded.

"You are now. Or I can take away the truck. Your only two choices."

"Fine. When do I start?"

"Monday."

Chase got to his feet. "Is that all? Can I leave now?"

Mr. Cooper nodded. "Be careful with what you decide to do, young man. There are consequences to your actions."

"Really? I know all about consequences. You're

barking up the wrong kid." He lifted his chin to me, and I got to my feet and followed him out. "It was her damn fault. She was double parked," he grumbled as we bolted out the door.

"Were you high?" I asked.

He gave me a vicious glare.

I took that as a yes. "Then it doesn't matter."

"Aren't you a ray of sunshine," he hissed.

"I'm only telling you the truth. Stop blaming other people for your problems and own it."

"Coming from the guy who owns up to his own dirty laundry."

"What is that supposed to mean?"

"You're hiding from Jay. Using Penny to make her jealous. Take your own damn advice and own it."

"I don't use people."

We were arguing just outside the truck, and he was already close to me. Real close. "You want me to help you be normal, remember? How is that not using *me*?" My eyes felt as if they wanted to fall out of my head. Chase looked so sad. But then he pulled away. "Get in the truck. I'll take you home."

ELIZABETH ARROYO

Chapter Seventeen

I fidgeted with my tie again. Mr. Harris usually did my ties at the funeral parlor. "Why do I have to wear a suit?" I called out to the kitchen from the bathroom where I dressed into one of my dark funeral suits. I wasn't having a particularly good day with what happened with Chase this morning. I had to stop myself four times from calling him. I didn't want to be a stalker friend.

"Jack is having guests over and I want to look nice," Vicky answered.

She did look nice. "You do look nice. But me." I gave up on my tie and met her in the kitchen.

Smiling, she took over my tie thing, looping it around to a perfect knot she slipped up to my throat. "There," she said, patting my tie. "Please. Just try."

I sighed.

Jack Johnson lived in a two level, four-bedroom home for just him and his son Finn. I couldn't help but notice that the number of rooms was perfect should Vicky marry him and we moved in. That is if they would want me too. Being a foster kid meant that I didn't belong anywhere. One word and I'd be back in a shelter. Though Vicky seemed to generally like me, Jack and Finn Johnson did not.

The house was nice, but Vicky always said it needed a woman's touch. I don't know what happened to the woman that birthed Finn and never drew up the nerve to ask. It wasn't like Finn and I were friends.

Vicky parked her car next to the sheriff's truck, and I carried the crock pot into the house. Jack greeted Vicky with a kiss and me with a smile. Okay, maybe he wasn't that bad.

"Kitchen." I announced my direction and headed that way. I had to pass the living room where Finn and Jaylene were sitting on the sofa. Neither of them even looked my way. The perfect couple. Stonelike and inanimate.

Vicky followed behind me and greeted the couple. I helped her in the kitchen while Finn and Jaylene stayed glued to the television. A few moments later, the doorbell rang, and Sheriff Johnson opened the door to Special Agent Nate Martinez who brought wine. I almost swallowed my tongue. My eyes bugged out of my head. I'd told him about stopping my meds. I was so busted. Special Agent Martinez must've sensed something because he smiled at me but didn't mention my name or knowing me right away.

The sheriff introduced him as Nate Martinez, a loan from New York, and not the FBI. Vicky smiled and seemed pleased. "This is my son, Jordan."

I always felt a tinge of warmth whenever she called me her son. A lie, but easier to explain then explaining that I was just a foster kid. "Nice to meet you," I said and shook his hand.

He went with it.

Dinner was awkward after that. I avoided Jaylene, which was hard to do since she was sitting directly in front of me. And I tried to ignore Nate, who was sitting at the edge to my left. Technically, I was just trying to disappear.

Finn talked about the upcoming homecoming game. Jaylene nodded and smiled at the exact perfect spots as if she'd rehearsed it. She probably had. I knew she was faking it. Except when she sneered my way. That was real.

"What college are you planning on going to?"

Special Agent Martinez asked Finn. Finn was a senior.

"Alabama University all the way." They broke out in cheers and whatever. I rolled my eyes. Special Agent Martinez caught me, and I could tell he was suppressing a smile.

"Jordan," Jaylene said, finally addressing me. Though the way she said my name, I knew it was something bad coming. "Where are *you* going to school?"

I wasn't going anywhere as fancy as Alabama University. My silence had Vicky bolting to action.

"Jordan has a few options," Vicky said, tapping my knee. "He still has time to decide." She gave me such a proud smile. I didn't want to ruin it with the truth. I was probably going to the local community college. I wasn't smart, athletic, or rich. Not many options in the schooling department when you didn't have at least one of the above. Then I glanced at Special Agent Martinez and, for some reason, I wanted him to be proud of me too.

"Maybe I'll try the military," I blurted.

Finn snorted. "They don't let loons in the military."

The room grew so silent I heard my ears ringing. Blood rushed to my pounding head.

"Finn," Vicky snapped and glared at Jack. *Say something*, that look said. Vicky had been defending me from bullies since she took me in. I'd been scrawny, awkward, broken like a baby bird freshly fallen from its nest.

"It's the truth, Vicky. The kid should have realistic options," Jack said.

A loon. Jaylene's smirk said it all. *You can't even fake normal. Not like me.*

I realized with a sense of dread that I had the steak knife clutched in my hand. All I had to do was reach out and stab Finn in the soft flesh at his neck and watch the blood drain out of his body. I wondered if he'd scream.

I turned to Special Agent Nate Martinez curiously watching me. He knew. He knew what I was thinking. What I wanted to do so bad.

I unclenched my fist under the table and heard the plink as the knife hit the floor. Then I shoved my chair back without saying anything and headed to the bathroom. I stopped in the hallway staring at the door. The closed door. The door with the knob.

"Don't open the door, Basil. Never open the door."

Something sank in my stomach. Maybe it was the realization that Finn was right. I was a loon, and I couldn't even fake otherwise.

Killer.

Monster.

I turned around and practically sprinted out the front door. Like mine, it had a window. It slammed behind me. I knew I wasn't normal. That truth hadn't bothered me before. It bothered me now. I didn't want to hurt anyone. I didn't want to become a monster. I hated the dark thoughts burrowing in my mind. I wanted to get them out. I wasn't a killer. I wasn't a monster.

I wasn't.

"Jordan, wait!" It was Vicky, and I heard her running after me. I kept walking. Just walking anywhere. "He's a jerk," she said as she came up on my left.

"I'm sorry," I said. "I'm sorry I'm not normal."

She grabbed my hand and stopped me, so we were facing each other. My tears were a horrible thing. I'd never felt them before. I'd never cried before. "I'd give anything to be normal. I would."

"Oh, honey. You're perfect."

I wasn't perfect though. There was something

wrong with me. I had a dark stain inside my soul. I would never be perfect.

Monday after school, I found myself inside Hector staring out into Mrs. Mills's field where Chase was working pulling weeds. He wore a thick coat and a beanie with his hair tucked inside. The cold was settling in quite nicely for this time of year. His lips moved and I knew he had his buds in, probably listening to one of his favorite bands. I owed him a sheepish apology for how I left things with him when he'd dropped me off at home after the corn freak-out.

I missed him.

I got out of the car and stood watching for a few moments before he even realized I was there staring at him like some sort of creeper. But he smiled at me so I couldn't have been that creepy. I took that as a hint to approach him.

"Hey," he said, his cheeks red from the cold. "What're you doing here?"

I shoved my hands in my pockets and shrugged. "Are we still friends?" I asked. I kicked at the hard dirt rather than look at him.

I heard him breathing harder as he fought with the cold ground. "Yeah, we're still friends. Why?"

The perfect athletic Finn going away to college made me think that Chase too had to have plans for college. "Where are you planning on going to college?"

Huffing, he dug the weed puller into the hard dirt paying attention to the plant struggling to stay alive in this cold but failing. "Yale, most likely. Why do you ask?"

"Just wondering."

He finally pulled it from the ground and shoved it into a plastic bag. Consigned that he'd done enough the thirty minutes he'd been out here freezing his ass off, he started for the barn and I followed. It was warmer and creepier in the barn. Lots of sharp things and old things. He pulled off his gloves, then the beanie, then the buds and wiped his nose. "What's really up? Something tells me you didn't come all this way to ask me about college in the freezing cold."

I started to lean against the old tractor when my elbow knocked a metal pole over. It clattered to the ground taking with it a slew of other metals that had been resting on the edge of the hood. I tried to save it but failed.

"Or maybe, you did," he said chuckling. "Just leave it. Come on, let's get out of here."

I ended up following Chase to a small café just at the outskirts of town. A hidden gem of a place with everything you would need to warm up. Hot cider, hot chocolate, cinnamon rolls, the works. Chase ordered for us and paid. We sat in a corner booth, and he shared a cinnamon roll with me. I ripped a piece and popped it into my mouth and almost died.

"This is so good."

He smiled as if satisfied that I loved it. It made me warmer than the hot chocolate he bought me. "I know right. My mom used to bring us here." His smile fell and he quickly turned his head to look out the window. "She loved the mountains."

I'd been here long enough that I didn't even really see the skyline filled with edges and loops anymore. But they were beautiful. "She doesn't love them anymore?" I asked, sipping the chocolate.

He turned and lowered his eyes to the cinnamon roll, breaking a piece and taking a slow bite. "So, college?" he said, changing the subject. "What are your plans?"

It was my turn to look anywhere but at him.

"What do you think about the military? I can go, right?"

He snorted and leaned back, eyes on me and I couldn't look away. "You'd be scary with a gun. Are you sure that's what you want to do?"

"You don't think I can handle a gun?"

"I think you can handle whatever you want, but would you want to?"

I lifted my eyes to his again, looking for the joke, for the *Yeah, right, you, a loon, in the military?* Something. Instead, he waited for my response. "I don't like guns."

"Exactly. Do something you'd actually like."

"I like to draw." I didn't say it so he could blush, but he blushed anyway probably remembering what I had drawn of him.

"Yeah, you're good at it." He lowered his eyes with a smile. The most adorable thing in the world. "Oh, here. Almost forgot." He dug into his coat pocket and pulled out my phone. "Liam found it."

I reached over to grab it, and our fingers brushed. We must've been charged because I felt an electric current run up my arm and settle somewhere in the pit of my stomach. My heart felt swollen. A lumpy, pulsing thing inside my chest. If he felt it too, he didn't show it. "Thanks," I mumbled and shoved it into my pocket.

Normal suddenly shattered with the realization that I didn't want to *be* like Chase. I wanted to kiss him.

ELIZABETH ARROYO

Chapter Eighteen

Crying babies were the worst. Penny had two of them. Twins. They hung off her mother as she tried to take pictures of us before we left for homecoming. Vicky had invaded poor Mrs. Cartwright's house and both mothers looked more comfortable than I felt. Penny wore a pale blue dress that shimmered. I wore a crusty suit with a pale blue tie to match. I had my change of clothes in my trunk.

A soft chime of her tiny bell bracelet sounded off our departure as she waved to her parents and Vicky. The one time I wouldn't have minded for Hector to fail me had been that moment when she and I were in the car, and she rolled her eyes. "You need a new car," she said.

Duh. I didn't say.

Hector didn't seem offended because he turned on without a sputter.

Thankfully, the weather had been nice enough that warming up had been fast. Penny spent the twenty-minute drive to the school on her cell phone with her friend, Marcy or Darcy, I couldn't tell. I tried to tune her out until she snorted. By the time we got to the school, I was ready to take a pill.

The school gym was decorated in pale fabrics and shimmering curtains. Strung up tea light made everything look as if we were under the real sky. We turned in our tickets, took more pictures with different backgrounds, and headed inside. A band played on stage, and I recognized Chase right away. He played the guitar and sang. I'd never seen him perform for an audience before. Whenever I was over at his house waiting for Jaylene, he'd invite me to his room to listen to him play. I didn't realize until that moment that I missed that too.

"Are you okay?" Penny asked.

I quickly averted my gaze, feeling—what? Guilty? Sad? I couldn't name what I felt at that moment. A loss too great for words. "Yeah," I lied because that was what normal people did. They lied.

"There's Aimee," Penny said.

"I'm going to get something to drink. You want something?"

"A juice would be fine."

I extracted my hand from hers and headed to the juice table manned, or rather womanned, by Mrs. Brainard, probably to make sure no one spiked the drinks. I bypassed the table and stood under shadow near the back wall closest to the stage just to catch my breath.

Who was I kidding? I couldn't do this. Being in a space with other people. I couldn't. Chase made a racket up on the stage and all I could do was stare at him. This was being a normal teenager at work? Really? I preferred to be at the funeral home with Mr. Harris or driving with Hector. This was a bit much.

Then Jaylene and Finn entered the hall as if already crowned king and queen. An entourage of football players and queen-bees strung up behind them. The team had won their homecoming game. Good for them. Everyone clapped and I watched as Jaylene put on her best face. The fake one with the fake smile that didn't quite reach her eyes. Her hands shook slightly but you wouldn't notice unless you knew what to look for. Her pulse throbbed as her heart raced, only noticeable if you looked at her pulsing carotid along her long delicate neck. She was an expert at faking things. Hell, she faked me into believing that we would always be friends.

"I still don't believe it."

My heart made a lunge up my throat at the sound

of Chase's voice behind me. I hadn't even noticed he stopped playing. I glanced at him over my shoulder as if he didn't spin the sun and moon for me. As if I didn't want him. I turned back to where Jaylene headed to her table with the beautiful people like her. I didn't add fuel to his statement. It wasn't a question anyway.

He didn't take the hint and took a closer step. This time our shoulders brushed, and I could smell his musk and sweat along with the peppermint. "I always thought you two would end up married with 2.5 kids, a dog, and a picket fence."

Still not a question.

He still didn't get the hint.

"So what was it about her that you didn't like?"

"She wasn't *you*," I blurted.

Just blurted. Out there. Words hanging between us. I was still staring at Jaylene in all her glory. Finn laughed it up as if he had the whole world in his hands for the taking. I felt Chase's overbearing presence beside me and realized, to my utter fucking humiliation, that I felt more at ease when I'd been skipping stones with him or shooting hoops. I felt more myself when we'd just sit and listen to music, sharing one bud each, our cheeks pressed together in his room.

I felt *longing*. That's the word. *Longing* for Chase Cooper.

He stood there, silent, until he walked away.

I didn't turn back to look where he walked to, though the compulsion was greater than the need to bury something. I rubbed my chest. My heart beating too fast made me breathless.

Normal. I had to be normal.

You're gay, Jordan. One more label threatening to topple your tower of normalcy.

"Pfft, what's so good about being normal

anyway?" I muttered, sure that talking to myself was not normal.

Fake it.

Just fake it.

I took a deep breath and headed for the juice table. I gathered two cups and walked to my date who looked rather appropriate for the event at hand. Aimee, the observant friend that she was, mouthed, *Are you okay?*

I answered with a fake smile I hoped looked real. I had to start working on my fake self before my real self took over and burned the world.

As far as dances went (not that I'd ever been to one), this one hadn't sucked. Aimee and Penny had been best friends since first grade, so they engaged each other, danced together too, until Aimee pulled a reluctant Riley to dance, and Penny pulled me out to dance. The floor thick with bodies, I just faked it. I was getting pretty good at this faking shit.

Hopping, sweating, swinging my date around worked pretty well and I actually had fun. Riley pulled me outside to get a breather and drink some booze from his cell phone shaped flask. Yeah, that was a thing.

The booze was nasty, and I had to swallow a few times to keep it down. I didn't want any more but Riley seemed to need more, and I didn't want him drunk. Especially since he had to drive too, so we split it fifty-fifty.

"What do you think about Penny?" he asked as he handed me the last of the liquor. At least two fingers worth. Being a good friend, I took it from him.

"She's nice."

"Pretty, right?"

I nodded, unsure where he was going with this line of thought. "Yeah."

"Are you going to try to…you know?"

I knew the *you know*, part. "I bought condoms," I said, and swallowed the rest of the booze. I wasn't going to try the *you know* with her but thought that wouldn't be normal to say out loud. I should be trying the *you know* with her if I wanted to be a normal boy, right? My head felt fuzzy about it.

He took the flask back, corked it, and shoved it into his pant pockets. "What about you and Aimee?" Thinking about him and Aimee felt weird. They were my best friends. It felt weird thinking about my best friends like that. I stopped thinking.

"She doesn't want to. Wants to wait until she's ready or some shit." He didn't sound so happy about it.

"Oh, that doesn't sound too bad."

He glared at me. "You're useless," he mumbled and walked back into the gym.

Prickly much? I almost called after him. At least you're not in love with a *guy*. I almost said. Was *I* in love with a guy?

I didn't want to think anymore.

Thinking sucked.

I walked back inside just as Jaylene and Finn took to the dance floor having been recently crowned. Shadows moved around her features making her look fragmented. Half of her lifted up with a smile, the other tempered with a frown. It felt unnerving.

"For someone who dumped her, you sure stare at her a lot," Aimee said beside me.

"Do not." Then I thought about all the times she passed by my locker and in the lunchroom when I couldn't stop myself from seeking her out. "Okay, maybe. There's just something off about her."

Aimee lifted both brows. "Like she's perfect, beautiful, with the in-crowd now?"

"No," I said with little conviction. "Like she's faking it. Like she's one nudge away from blowing up. You should've heard her threatening Penny."

"I heard she threatened you."

"Trust me. If I were Penny, I'd hide somewhere and never show my face."

Aimee gave me her yeah right look. "Speaking of, where is your date and where is my date? I seemed to have lost them."

I shrugged. Didn't really care. "I was outside with Riley just now."

Aimee patted my shoulder, then leaned into my ear. "Don't forget to have fun and stop staring at other people having fun, mister."

I rolled my eyes, but she was already gone.

Stop staring at other people having fun, Jordan.

Great advice. I should be living. Dancing with my date, making out, doing things. I didn't want to be alone forever. Even Chase had a girlfriend who he was arguing with at the exact same spot I told him I wanted to be him. Or I wanted him. I couldn't be sure what I'd said. Didn't matter. Tabatha finally had enough and tried to swallow him whole. She fisted his shirt as if hanging on for dear life. Their heads moved, their lips pressed, and sometimes their tongues made an appearance.

I looked away. I wanted to experience a first kiss with someone who would want me like that. I wanted to be reckless. I wanted…I wanted to be stupid normal. Not perfect normal. Stupid normal. My whole world suddenly seemed unfair because I couldn't even manage *that*.

The reason I preferred Jaylene. Because she knew all about being different. Not having behavior patterns that fit the norm. She knew what it felt like to be misunderstood. Like me. But unlike me, she hid it better.

Aimee was right. I had to stop staring at her.

Especially as she walked toward me with those shadows on her face making it hard to decide if I should run or smile at her. Blue expressionless eyes made me unable to move. "Dance with me," she said, taking my cold hands in her warm ones.

The music changed to something slow. The Deejay had taken over, giving Chase time to snog his girlfriend. Was snog even a word? It rhymed with snot, which was pretty gross.

Jaylene stopped in the middle of the dancefloor right under the disco ball overhead. I scanned the faces in the room, all watching us. Especially Finn who looked like he wanted to pummel me. I turned back to Jaylene. A prism of lights circled us as if we were in a fairytale. She lifted her arms around my neck. I planted my hands on her hips, and we swayed.

"I don't think your boyfriend is happy that we're dancing," I said.

"I don't care."

I believed her. Jaylene never cared what anyone thought about her so long as she had her shit together. And honestly, dancing was nice.

"I saw your girlfriend leave with Riley," she said, arching a perfectly trimmed brow.

"She's not my girlfriend," I said quickly.

"Apparently not. She was sucking Riley's tongue. How does that make you feel?"

I blinked away my confusion. "Riley's with Aimee. He wouldn't—"

She leaned forward, brushing her lips against my ear. "He did it because that's all these fake people want. A boy wants a girl to put out. A girl wants a handsome, strong boy to put in. They don't care about emotions. They all want to be like *us*."

My heart started its rapid pace again. "And what

are we?"

Her full lips curled in a smile. "We are divinity. The world is ours to make how we see fit. You'll see."

I waited for the punchline. The snark, the sass, the wink. All I got was someone checked out of reality. Chills ran through my body. Then, just before the song ended, she leaned into me. I startled back, meeting her nefarious smirk. This one did reach her eyes, and it made me cold all over.

Chapter Nineteen

Aimee: **I went home. Penny could have him!!**

I wanted to slaughter Riley. Jaylene smirked my way as she wrapped her arms around Finn. *I told you so*, written all over that smirk.

"Hey." I jolted, fumbled with my phone, and dropped it. Liam chuckled and plucked it off the floor. "Are you okay?" He handed me the phone

I snatched the phone from his hand. "You should stop creeping up on people."

"Wasn't creeping." The corner of his lips lifted in a half-quirky smile that must've worked on girls or guys. With Liam, I wasn't sure. He'd never had a girlfriend and I'd never seen him with a dude at school. Though rumors did travel that he preferred dudes. "Hey." He snapped his fingers in front of my face to bring me back to the present. I blinked the haze away. "You're so off, dude. Your eyes get like, dead." His smile remained.

No one had ever told me about my eyes turning dead, and I really didn't have a comeback for that one, so I just narrowed my dead eyes at him. "Why are you even talking to me? You've been angry at me since I failed to get information on Natalia," I sneered at him and almost added, *hmmm*.

He looked admonished by my words. "Yeah, sorry about that." He shrugged. "Looks like you need a friend." Because not only had Jaylene dumped me, so had Penny and the whole school already knew about it. "Are you going to Quinn's? The after party is going to be there."

"Are you inviting me to Quinn's?" I realized the moment those words slipped out how pathetic I sounded.

As if I were looking for a date or something. I was not looking for a date, or something.

The mistake registered because Liam narrowed the already small gap between us. "Are you asking me to ask you on a date?"

My tongue suddenly felt as if I'd walked a marathon. In the Sahara Desert. "Uh."

A soft touch at my waist had me looking down to Liam's hands on me. Touching me. "Maybe we should dance first."

Vocabulary left me and my words strung together like cheese soup. "Mfhugh, duh." Or at least that's what my word sounded like while my face turned beet red.

"Hey, Liam! We're heading out! You coming?" Ash yelled as if Liam weren't just five feet in front of him. Liam startled, pulling away from me as if just realizing we were still in the school gym dancing in a corner. "Yeah," he said, then turned to me and winked. "I'll see you there, yeah?"

Instead of just leaving he waited for my verbal response. "Yeah," I managed.

Still with that smile that seemed to tug something inside my chest, he jogged out of the gym to meet his bandmates.

Why did all the creeps have to be so cute?

Sitting inside Hector, I thought I should go make sure Aimee was okay. I should strangle Riley for taking my date and for hurting Aimee. Instead, I drove to Quinn's. Normal meant being a selfish, reckless asshole who wanted to experience his first house party and maybe flirt some more with a certain boy. Though Liam didn't make me feel all tingly the way Chase did, Liam had to be gay and maybe, unlike Chase, he'd want to be with me. I didn't have to like *like* a boy to kiss him. Right?

Quinn's house sat off road in a two-acre lot. Except for cars parked everywhere, you'd think the place was abandoned. No parking, I had to leave Hector off the main road and sprint to the house because it was cold, and I left my coat in the car. I should've brought my bag of clothes to change, but I left that too. As soon as I opened the door, I was flooded with loud music and noise. Apparently, his parents were out of town. I recognized some of the people from school and there wasn't the usual hierarchical structure like during lunch. The jocks laughed with the weebs. The music geeks with the cheerleaders. Everyone seemed relaxed, even my best friend snogging my girlfriend in a corner. The asshole.

Back near the dining room window, Monkey Swine played a song that had the house buzzing. Chase and Liam looked really good together and even shared the mic to sing. My heart stilled as Chase seemed to spear his laser vision right through me. I felt it like a touch and my whole body broke out in a warm blossom of heat that sizzled my skin. The connection lasted a second before his eyes found something else.

It's just your imagination.

But a boy could dream.

The band finished their set and Liam, not Chase, made a straight line for me. I couldn't help but to give him the attention he deserved. Liam was handsome. He was kinda nice. Had also protected me that day from Steel. And I did feel a kind of buzz coming from our narrow distance. Or it could've been just him buzzing with adrenaline from the set.

"You made it," he said and placed his hand just over my head against the wall and leaned in. I turned my head figuring he probably wanted to whisper something in my ear. Not kiss me in a room full of people. Even I knew the gay thing could be a problem. "Does this mean we're on a date?"

I placed my hand on his sweaty shirt feeling his heart beating fast. "Ugh, you didn't drive me here, so I think no."

His face was close enough to see the small freckles on the bridge of his nose. There was something else. Something familiar in his eyes. We stared at each other, and this wasn't like a staring contest to see who would blink first. This was like trying to remember something I'd lost.

He blinked and pulled back, taking my hand in his. "Come on. I need a drink."

We slipped into the kitchen where he proceeded to serve me a blue liquid in a red cup. "I see your pretty Penny found a smiley Riley." He pressed his full lips together then we both started laughing. "What?" he said, sounding offended. "I couldn't come up with anything else for Riley." He handed me the cup. "Try this. You'll forget about them."

I drank it and almost coughed up a lung. "Is this what normal people drink?"

He arched his brow. "Don't insult me by calling *me* normal."

I licked my lips and noticed that he noticed. "I thought normal was good."

He snorted. "Who told you that?" He ran his thumb along my bottom lip. It was then I noticed that he was swaying a little bit. Slurring his words. Liam Grant was drunk. "No, let me guess. Your mother told you that."

I couldn't quite move and without thinking, really without thinking, I grazed the pad of his thumb with my tongue. His pupils seemed to swallow the blue of his eyes. His beautiful eyes. As if in a trance, he scanned every inch of my face. My heart crashed against my chest. I was going to either pass out or lose it any minute now.

He looked at me. Really looked into my eyes. "You have very beautiful eyes, Jordan," he said.

Yup. Lost it. Completely.

Liam started to lean into me, cupping my face with one hand, the other caging me against the wall at my back. I usually didn't like being touched, but this was different. Welcomed. His eyes lowered to my lips and the space between us narrowed. He was going to kiss me. I was going to kiss a guy! A cute guy who was into dudes. Who thought my eyes were beautiful!

"Hey."

The voice made us both startle, but Liam didn't release me as if he didn't care who saw us kissing. He just turned his head to Chase.

"Quinn is looking for you, asshole," Chase said, angrily.

Liam looked pissed. Chase looked pissed too. Liam turned to me and leaned in. His lips skimmed mine. I wanted the kiss. I did. Then he stumbled back.

"What the fuck, Coop?"

Chase had pulled him away from me. "You're drunk. Go drink some water and leave Jordan alone."

I didn't want him to leave me alone, but no one seemed to be paying attention to me.

Liam poked Chase in the chest. "Why? It's not like *you* have the balls to make a move."

Chase turned so red I thought he was going to hit Liam. Liam smirked. Knew something I did not that had Chase fleeing the scene. Leaving me. I quickly grabbed a bottle of water just to do something. What did Liam mean make a move? Chase wanted to make a move on who? I realized my brain felt fuzzy. Not like a full fuzzy, more like a warped fuzzy. I drank too much. "Liam, he's right.

Drink some water." I opened it for him and watched as he reluctantly drank some. Then he wiped his lips.

"He broke up with Tabatha tonight," Liam said, glaring at me as if that had been my fault. "Are you into him?"

I opened my mouth unsure what I'd meant to say. Certainly, not, "Yeah. I…I like him."

Liam snorted. "Well, you better make the first move. He never will."

Liam left me pondering that little bomb.

Chase broke up with Tabatha. Make the first move. He never will. Was Chase into me? Did he like me? Hope and recklessness, more recklessness and maybe the booze in my blood, had me sprinting after Chase. I saw him with Jaylene. He said something to her, and she slapped him. I winced. "I love you too, sis," I heard him growl out just before he rushed outside. I gave Jaylene a wide berth. I wasn't that brave.

The cold wind bit at my exposed skin. Chase had parked away from the crowd, under an old birch. Hidden. I wasn't going to make it before he left. "Chase," I called. I didn't want to think. I left all reasonable thought at Quinn's.

Chase looked sad and I hated the red handprint Jaylene had left behind on his face. He didn't deserve that. I wanted to protect him. I wanted to see him smile, make him laugh. I wanted to kiss him.

So I did.

Chapter Twenty

I didn't stop moving until I slammed my mouth against his and his back hit the truck. Maybe, I should've asked first. Too late. I felt him stiffen, but then his mouth opened, and he was kissing me! His hands tangled into my hair, pulling me in closer. His tongue doing things to mine as I tried to catch up. My first kiss scorched through my veins, and I pressed against him. I wanted, no, needed more of him. I chased the kiss as if we were the last two people on the planet. Chase melted into my arms and moaned. Moaned into my mouth. I never wanted to part. But a car speared us with its headlights for a moment and Chase went stiff. Then he pushed me hard. I tripped on my shaky feet and fell on my ass. He wiped his lips. Wiped me off him like I was some disgusting piece of shit. Realizing what he'd just done, he looked horribly guilty.

"Jordan." He reached for me, but I slapped his hand away.

Tears stung my eyes. A wedge lodged itself in my throat. The world started to spin. The night sky behind Chase too close. I got to my feet, hoping he'd say something else. Like, I'm sorry. I'm not into you. Like *something*. He said nothing. I think that was the worst part.

I shoved my hands in my pocket. "I'm sorry," I managed. I couldn't look at him. "I shouldn't have done that. I—just thought. I'm sorry." I couldn't dig my own grave, though I wanted to at that moment.

He still didn't say anything, and I walked away. I didn't look back. I brushed my tears from my face and bypassed the house to Hector. Thankfully, I parked far enough that no one could see me. Away from the noise, the crowd. I shouldn't have come. And why the tears? In my whole damn life, I hadn't cried this much. I attributed that fact to my meds. I needed to get back on them so I would feel nothing. Numbness was better than this shit stabbing me from the inside out. I rather be abnormal than normal.

I should've been paying attention. I should've. But I didn't see the threat until I was slammed against my door. I dropped my keys, and Miller plucked them up with a wicked grin on his face before he opened the trunk.

Steel held me from behind making sure I couldn't run.

The blood drained from my body. Did they see what I'd done? The kiss? Chase? Would they rat us out? I knew in my bones that Chase would throw me under the bus and that humiliation would kill me.

"I know what you're afraid of," Steel whispered into my ear.

His words didn't match my current mindset. Not until I realized he wasn't talking about the kiss. He was talking about something worse.

The rest was a blur of movement. I felt hands on my feet as they lifted me up. I tried to scream, but Steel clamped his hand around my mouth. It took some contorting, but they shoved me into the trunk and slammed it shut. The small space turned from a trunk to a grave. They'd dropped me inside a grave. I don't know how long I screamed and pounded the trunk for. It could've been minutes, could've been hours. Until my fists hurt, my eyes hurt, and I couldn't breathe. I heard someone try to start Hector. An argument. Two voices, raised. I started pounding again, screaming. Hector wouldn't start and whoever they were left.

The sawing in and out of my breath was the only sound in the cramped space. My heart pounded furiously behind my chest. Tears prickled my eyes. My vision blurred and I shut them trying to find my safe place in my head. But there was nothing there. I wasn't safe. I'd never be safe. And I started to cry.

"Basil, don't cry," someone in the darkness said.

"I don't want to be buried," I managed to choke out.

"It'll only be for a little while. I promise."

I believed the voice. The familiarity of it burrowed somewhere deep in my heart. A voice with no name, no face. Only a feeling that I could trust him. "Why me? What about Kale? They'll hurt him."

"I'll protect him until you bring the cops. I promise. You have to do this. For them." He handed me Teddy and I clutched onto him tight. *"Don't forget to run. Nana will be with you, but you have to run."*

"Sage," I whispered. The name, like Kale's name, felt right. Memories struggled to surface but I could only remember the cold feeling of the corpse on me. A boy telling me what to do. Our dog. The images swirled in my mind like dust motes. I couldn't catch them. They'd dissolve or disappear when I tried. But they were real. I felt it deep in my bones, that these memories were real. The boy who buried me had been real. Kale had been my brother. I needed to be brave. I needed to save them. It meant waiting for the rain.

I closed my eyes at some point and must've fallen asleep because when I opened them, the trunk was slightly open. The voice in my head was silent. Wincing back the pain from being folded for so long, I pushed it fully and rolled out, falling hard on the gravel. The flush of cool air made me shiver and the biting pain on my palms and knees made me wince. Sometime between

Steel manhandling me and this moment, I had pissed myself.

It was still dark out only now it was so quiet. I may have been the last person left alive in the world. I considered staying on the ground and waiting for someone to find me, but the embarrassment of having them know I pissed myself had me swallowing the wedge in my throat and ignoring the pain. I got to my feet. I slid inside my car. My phone had been tossed into the passenger seat and the keys had been left inside the ignition. When I turned the key Hector didn't even make a peep. When I picked up my phone, it was dead too.

I would've laughed if I didn't feel so terrible.

I hated this car. I hated my life! I wanted to scream. I didn't. Instead, I breathed and shoved all the unwanted emotions to the dark pit behind my heart. Feelings sucked. I reverted to analyzing things. Separating the pieces from the whole. I had to get home. I had no phone and no car. The party had died sometime while I'd been asleep in the trunk. There were no cars in front of Quinn's place. The lights were off. He was probably crashed. I was pretty sure I could go inside and call someone. But who would I call? Vicky was working nights, and I wasn't going to call Jack fucking Johnson so he could smell the piss on me. The *loon.*

Frustrated, I changed out of my wet pants and into the jeans I'd brought. Cold as shit, my teeth took thirty seconds to start chattering. I shoved the emergency roadside kit into my bag and shrugged into my puffer coat, beanie, and gloves before getting out of the car.

I was *done.*

Hector could go to hell with the rest of them.

I could walk the trail and make it home before daylight. Moving helped my jittery nerves. Walking helped clear my head. I felt fuzzy, nothing clear. I shouldn't have stopped the medication. I shouldn't have listened to Riley. I shouldn't have kissed Chase. I couldn't stop crying now and it only made me colder.

Don't cry, Basil. You have to be brave. Can you be brave?

I shook the voice out of my head. I wasn't brave. I was nothing.

I walked, my body trembling. I'd never feel warm again.

I don't know how long I'd walked for when headlights cut through the night. I recognized the sheriff's truck. If I were smart, I would've flagged him down, pled with him to take me home. I wasn't smart. I ducked into the thick cover of trees until it sped past. Too fast, in my opinion. It wasn't like the sheriff was chasing anything down. There was no one out in the streets this time of night. Well, no one with any brain cells. I started down the path again when I thought the coast was clear.

Big mistake.

Once I stepped back into the street, the sound of skidding brakes drew my attention back to the truck. It made a sharp U-turn. Its high beams blinded me the closer it got, and it was moving fast. In four seconds, I was going to be roadkill. Sheriff Johnson wanted me dead.

After the dinner disaster, Vicky had ended things with him. He blamed me and now wanted me out of the picture for good. I ducked back into the woods and ran. The truck slammed to a stop and a few seconds later, I heard a door slam and movement behind me. At this point, I couldn't see two feet in front of me, but neither could he.

Basil, calm your breathing. Measure your steps. Use your other senses to see.

I slammed my shoulder against a tree and bit back

a cry. Using my hands, I moved around it for cover and dropped low to the ground. I couldn't see anything, but I heard the shift in the trees, the crunching of ground and leaves, and breathing that wasn't mine. Then a flash of light cut the darkness directly to my right. I held my breath. The light beam swung left, then right for a few seconds before whoever it was decided I was not worth the effort. He cut the lights, leaving us in perfect darkness. Smart. With the light off, I couldn't even get a glimpse of his size. I must've been hugging that tree for several more minutes until I heard the truck take off. It was only then that I could take a deeper breath. I leaned my forehead against the rough bark of the tree.

What the hell had just happened? Had it really been Sheriff Johnson? I was left with more questions than I had the mental capacity to pick apart right now. I just wanted to go home. End this nightmare.

Something brushed over my foot, and I squealed, stumbling back. The dark forest came alive. The shifting of earth and leaves heightened my sense of self preservation.

Run, Basil. Run.

The surge of adrenaline that rammed through me had me forgetting every danger I knew about the woods. Namely, don't run in the dark. The uneven terrain could end in a broken leg or worse. I could crash headfirst into a tree and break open my head like a melon. But every danger seemed secondary to my need to leave whatever happened behind me.

The sound of water gave me a clue to where I was heading—the various cave systems that shouldn't be navigated at night because of—

I slipped and hit the ground hard. The momentum had my body tumbling down a steep slope.

"Family. It means we protect each other. Your job

is to come back so nothing happens to Kale."

A scream tore out of my throat as I flailed in an effort to stop my descent as memories spiraled inside my brain. Memories I had buried.

For a fleeting second, I felt nothing but air under me. Then pain. Then nothing.

ELIZABETH ARROYO

Chapter Twenty-One

"Sage, I'm scared."

"Just close your eyes, Basil. And you won't see the monster."

The echo of voices floated in and out of my consciousness.

I lifted back into the world in slow pulsing waves. I risked movement. First wiggling my toes, moving my ankles, my legs. Then my arms and my fingers. Nothing bent awkward, no burst of pain awakened with me. I opened my eyes and blinked a few times to see that I was staring at dirt. Slowly, I pulled myself up on all fours, listening to the buzzing around the world, unable to focus. My vision was hazy, my mind groggy. I climbed to my feet using the dirt wall as my support. Though nothing seemed broken, I had enough scrapes and bruises to make me wince. I wiped my forehead, and my fingers came away sticky and wet.

I waited, figuring the world would right itself soon. I just needed to keep myself on my feet.

Basil.

The whispered name made me stiffen. The hairs on my body stood on end.

Basil. Don't move. Don't cry. You're dead. The dark can't hurt you.

The voice silenced and the world came into focus. I'd fallen down a hole and into one of nature's great wonders. A fucking cave. There were a bunch of them near the falls. I was such an idiot to head this way. I should've known. Mountains and caves, oh my! Still dark, because it was already late fall. The days got shorter as the temperature dropped. If I didn't get out of here, I was going to die. If I didn't build a shelter with fire, I was going to die. If I didn't get my shit together, I was going to die. I fell on my ass and hugged my knees.

I tracked the time in my head. Still dark, it had to be early morning on Sunday. I had a flashlight and my bag when I fell. I still had the bag with me. And I'd either lost the flashlight, or it got busted on the way down because there was no break in the darkness. I'd have to wait until morning. Meant, I had to stay warm. I pulled out the emergency kit Vicky had bought me with the car—since, you know, Hector left me everywhere, and found a small shovel, bandages, a lighter, a multi tool knife, a thermal blanket and a penlight inside. "Thank you, Vicky."

I turned on the penlight. It was enough to see a few feet in front of me. The night temperature dropped to at least forty. I'd fallen on a cushy part of a small incline and had rolled to the bottom. The hole above me had to be at least twenty feet above my head. It spilled a few sprinkles of light but not much to help. I'd been lucky I didn't break my neck or pop a bone through the skin. That would've sucked.

I climbed to my feet and stretched, the pain superficial but my predicament real. Whereas normal people would've probably panicked and feared the unknown darkness, I didn't. My brain started to see the problem and pull on the threads that might save my life.

I had to figure out a way out of here. Or try to find something like those wilderness people do when they're lost in the woods. Vicky had enrolled me in Orphan's are Us, or at least that's what Simon Thompson called it. A camp where they'd take foster kids into the woods and teach us how to survive as if they knew I'd end up needing the skills they taught because I was a total idiot. I knew how to build a fire pit. I knew how to conserve energy and all about hypothermia. Relevant to my current predicament.

I decided to explore my surroundings to make sure there weren't any predators in the cave. Mr. Sorenson, one of the camp counselors, had said that Montana had become the land of the wild animals. That wasn't a comforting thought right now. The only sounds inside the cave were the muted echoes of the night critters above me. And my breathing.

I swung the light in front of me, but I still couldn't get my bearings. The penlight was too small. It forced me to move from my place near the wall. The muddied ground squished under me, but it meant water. I walked a few yards when the light landed on a rolled rug. Maybe someone had used the cave before and left some things behind. That gave me a semblance of hope. Perhaps an exit. I could be home before Vicky got home from work. She'd never know what happened to me. That I pissed myself. I'd go back to Quinn's and burn Hector where I left it.

I was thinking about the tinder I would use to light my car on fire when I reached the rug. I dropped on my knees and planted my hand on the underside, feeling for the seam until I found it. It was thick and looked intact. I could use it for shelter if I needed to. Pushing it until it rolled on its flat side required more strength than I thought it should've. I bit the end of the flashlight to keep the light in front of me as I rolled it back with two hands, exposing not only the topside of a rug but also a face. A human face.

Penny Cartwright.

The narrow beam caught on her pale throat. Slowly, I trailed the light up to her face. Her skull had been crushed. Hair matted with blood, bone, and gunky stuff I didn't want to think about, stuck out between the red strands. Blood soaked into the rug, but not enough to suggest she'd been killed on the rug. The rug had been just a tool to get rid of the body. Her eyes were open, glazed in death. And her skin was chilled but not cold. She couldn't have been dead long.

I'd never been afraid of the dead. The dead couldn't hurt you. But this was different. I had felt something for Penny. A tug just behind my sternum. I'd just been with her a few hours ago. I'd seen her sucking faces with Riley.

Oh, God. Riley.

The thought of my best friend being dead sent the first burst of fear rushing through me. I crawled away from Penny in a panic and swept the light left and right, searching for another lump that could be a body. My heart raced inside my chest. The throb pulsed in my temple. Not that I didn't care about Penny. No one deserved to be murdered—which duh, her being in a cave, wrapped in a rug meant she'd been murdered. But Riley was my best friend, and I didn't want to lose him even if he had stolen the one girl who had a crush on me from me. Though, that would imply that Penny hadn't wanted to kiss Riley too. You couldn't steal a person. That would be kidnapping, and Riley wasn't a kidnapper. He was an unfaithful cheater. Not a kidnapper. And I hadn't wanted to kiss Penny anyway. I had wanted to kiss Liam, but then Chase...

I shut my eyes and ran a trembling hand over the lump on my head, wincing at the pain. I didn't want to think about Chase or Liam. Or Riley as a cheater. I didn't want to think about Steel, the trunk. I didn't want to think of my wet pants on the driver's seat. How if I died here, someone would know I peed myself. Chase would know. I didn't want to think about Penny dead.

I forced my eyes to open. Thankfully, I didn't find

another body. I didn't find anything. A breath of relief sprung loose followed by a bit of guilt. As the adrenaline rush subsided, I managed to crawl back to Penny and covered her face again before moving back to my wall.

My wall.

As if an invisible barrier had been erected between me and the dead. Maybe that's how I was able to work with Mr. Harris and the dead bodies. Special Agent Nate Martinez's question cycled through my head. *How could you do this type of work?*

Because subconsciously I had built an invisible barrier between me and the dead.

I should've probably been freaking out. I knew a normal kid, even Chase, would freak out to be amid a fresh murder. Tainting forensic evidence. Maybe the killer was still around.

I didn't want to die. Not like Natalia Montenegro. Not like Penny Cartwright. Not like the others behind the door. I knew I should be prepping for my survival and not thinking about useless things. But I felt so damn tired.

I spread the thermal blanket open and wrapped it around my body like a burrito. I dropped on my side, curled into a ball, and closed my eyes.

Tired.

So damn tired.

I'll figure it out when the sun comes out.

The sun came out in what felt like minutes after I'd closed my eyes. I got to my feet and stretched my sore body. Everywhere hurt. But at least I was alive. I sheepishly looked over at Penny. "Sorry, Penny," I said. She didn't respond.

The cave room I'd fallen into was about fifteen paces in a rectangle. The limestone walls of the cave were slick. Which reminded me that I needed to find water. Stalactites hung like stilettos from the ceiling.

They looked menacing and I imagined the ceiling crushing down on me, skewering me in place. I shuddered. Climbing to the hole in the ceiling wasn't a feasible escape. But neither was exploring the cave with no sense of direction. I could get stuck between two walls and die a slow hungry death. The hole above me was my escape. I just had to figure out how. Scaling the wall wasn't an option. I'd probably break my neck. I screamed for help until I tasted blood at the back of my throat.

I had a few precious hours before the sun dipped to the west and fell out of sight. My eyes went back to Penny. She had a purse with her. A coat too. And the rug.

Shit. Shit.

The itch to bury her felt so damn strong I had to clench my hands into fists. "We'll bury you the right way, okay?" I said as I approached her. "But I need to know if you have something that can help me get out of here. Like a phone. A charged phone."

I took a deep inhale and unwrapped her completely. The rug was thick enough that I could probably make an enclosure if I had to stay another night. Ignoring the blood on it, I rolled it up and set it aside. I'd dealt with dead bodies before. Mr. Harris taught me what happens during death and decomposition. He even taught me anatomy and some causes of death in the bodies we'd worked on. Penny's cause of death had to be blunt trauma to the head. Her eyes were open and glazed. She was in the autolysis stage, her body still malleable. I maneuvered her out of her coat and tossed that to the side, then I found her purse.

"Please. Please," I chanted but didn't know what I was exactly pleading for. Her phone rested on its side with an external charger. My heart jumped with hope at the sight of it. I pulled out the phone and it flashed on demanding a password. But it didn't matter because there was no damn signal. Of course not. I grumbled and used her stiff thumb to unlock the phone and delete the option for a password. I could use it as a light source or a brick. Something. I shoved it into my pocket. I also found a half-filled small water bottle. I sipped the water, wetting my dry lips and parched throat. I wanted to drink it all, but I knew better. Because no one was coming for me.

Panic finally settled into the pit of my stomach, and I started to call out again, despite my ruined voice. Hikers often walked the trails near the caves. Maybe someone would hear me. I called out until I couldn't anymore then I cried.

ELIZABETH ARROYO

Chapter Twenty-Two

I fell asleep and woke up to the sun at the edge of the hole, throwing shadows everywhere. I quickly gathered what I could for a fire, which wasn't much. I went back to Penny, apologized for taking her small notebook from her purse but explaining that I needed it for kindling, and went back to my wall. Ten minutes later, I had a small fire going, warming up the small space. Then I went to work with the rug, sticking it into the rock face like a fabric lean-to making sure the blood faced out. I knew I was tampering with evidence, but it was all I had. Live and worry about forensic evidence later or die and become evidence. "Sorry, Penny," I muttered. "I'm so damn sorry."

I'd always run a touch above freezing, but this cold burrowed into my bones. I had a ration of water, but no food. Under the rug enclosure, wrapped in my thermal blanket, I heard things. Insects crawling around. I hated bugs. I hated the cold. I hated all of this. "Sage, what's happening?" I whispered. I shut my eyes and waited for an answer that did not come.

It's going to be okay. Someone will come. Someone will.

I woke up to frigid air. I sipped some of the water just to wet my tongue. The fire had died out during the night. I pulled the rug back and Penny continued to stare at me as if it'd been my fault she had to witness my attempt to survive.

"It's not my fault you're here. You left with Riley." I didn't want to admonish her or blame her for her current predicament of being dead, but she had been Aimee's friend. She had been my date, and she cheated on me even before we really got started. And thinking of that, made me think about Riley. Was he too in some sort of hole or dead?

Don't ask questions for which you are not prepared to hear the answers for, Jordan. Vicky would say. Thinking about Vicky made my chest hurt. Maybe she'd be relieved. Maybe she'd cry. Maybe she'd blame herself at failing to save me.

In the cold, I did some exercise to get my blood flowing and stretched. I searched the cave and found no way out or a food source, but I did find wet stones. I followed the small drip to its source and made a small divot to catch water in the water bottle. It took hours to fill, but it was something.

"At least we'd be buried," I told Penny. She didn't have an opinion one way or another.

As I sat with nothing but her to look at, I wondered what special items I could bring to her funeral. Penny liked charms. She had a bracelet with a small bell on her wrist when I'd picked her up for homecoming. I didn't see it on her now. Maybe she lost it when she'd been murdered. I'd make sure to buy her a new one and put it on her wrist at the funeral.

Then I thought about the boy. Sage.

The memory of the boy struggled to solidify, but like a drop of water on a vast ocean, it rippled until it became diluted. I knew the boy was real. I knew the warning in my heart that something terrible had happened to him, to me, to the others, was real. But I had nothing solid. It was all a feeling in my gut. I pushed the thoughts out of my mind and curled into a ball under the rug, refusing to think of the blood, of the dying fire. Of my death in this place.

That night was the coldest of my life.

The next day came, and the next. The fire died

down and I had no strength to build another. No longer sure how long I'd been trapped in that cave, I found I no longer cared. At least not until I heard a slight ping and felt something vibrate in my pocket. I pulled out the offending device. Penny's phone.

As I lay on my side, tucked into the thermal blanket, I put the phone to my ear.

"Hello?"

I recognized the voice on the other end. A rush of hope settled in the pit of my stomach that he'd save me like he promised. "Dad?" My voice came out small and weak.

"Son, thank God you're alive. I need you to tell me where you are."

I shook my head. Or I thought I shook my head. I didn't feel myself move at all. "I don't know where I'm at. I don't want to die." And then I started to cry, only no tears came out. "Puh-lease," I stammered, my teeth chattering. "Don't hang up."

The man on the other side of the phone sounded desperate. "I'm not going to hang up. I promised you, remember?"

I did remember. When I had found the adults, they had contacted the police. My father came for me. He had held me. I remembered he smelled of cinnamon and vanilla. I remember his strong arms holding me as he promised to keep me safe. "I remember," I whispered.

"You have to stay awake, son. You have to survive this."

I wiped my nose. I didn't want to disappoint the man on the other end of the call, but I didn't know what to do to survive anymore. "I'm so cold, Dad. I'm so cold."

"It's the hypothermia setting in. You have to get up. You need to hydrate."

"I didn't do anything wrong," I cried into the phone, too tired to even move. "I tried, but it didn't work."

"Where are you?"

I shut my eyes. They burned. *Where are you, Basil? You need to tell the cops so they can save them.*

"Save who? They're all dead. I couldn't save any of them." I opened my eyes and knew what I'd see beyond the rug I'd used to hide. The dead. Just like beyond the door. "I fell. Near Pike's Pass. It's a cave."

"Are you alone?" His voice started to crack. The connection was unstable.

"No," I managed to say. "She needs to be buried. All dead things need to be buried."

"Bury the memories, baby. It's better this way," my mom had said. I didn't know how I knew it was her, but I *knew*. She had left me in a small apartment with a woman. *"I'll be back, Rosa. A day."*

Rosa, the woman holding my hand, nodded.

But Mom never came back.

I remembered the boy. He was black with big round brown eyes. That was important. The eyes are what catches prey. The Parent had said. All of my brothers and sisters had beautiful eyes.

I curled myself into a tighter ball to keep warm.

I shook my head. I don't have brothers and sisters.

But I did.

I do.

I remembered them, us. Trying to survive. *Stay away from the doors. Never open them.*

And then screams.

I screamed and screamed. Then I started to think some more. I thought about Natalia and the scar. Family. The scar meant family. We protect our own. Did Penny have a scar? Was that why she was dead? I hadn't checked. Too late. I thought about Chase silently suffering in that house. He hid all the ugly so well. But I'd seen it. And I thought he liked me.

Liam had been wrong.

The world collapsed into one point in my brain revealing to me the little boy I had been. Broken. Afraid of doors. Compelled to dig graves. The scar that made me part of a family. And death.

Sometimes they die.

I heard barking in the distance.

Wait for Nana to come get you and then run, Basil. Run.

I had to dig myself out to save them. I pushed the rug out of the way. My feet shook. My body was so cold. I used the wall to get to my feet. My tongue was heavy, my throat dry. "Nana! I'm here!" I cried. "Don't leave me! Please!" I tasted blood in my throat. Heard more barking, then dirt fell around me.

"Jordan!"

I looked up at Mrs. Brainard peering down into the hole at me. The most beautiful person I'd ever seen in my life. And then I passed out.

ELIZABETH ARROYO

Chapter Twenty-Three

Three days, twenty-one hours, and thirty-six minutes. The time I spent in that cave. Buried. A team at the hospital carefully took my clothes and put them in individual bags. They swabbed my scratches, inside my cheek, and under my fingernails. And they weren't doctors. I heard Vicky arguing with the cops outside my door and I slid my eyes to Special Agent Martinez who watched silently as the FBI processed me. That's the word they used. They even took some of my hair.

Finally, they allowed Vicky back inside as the doctors addressed my hypothermia with heavy heated blankets, and an IV in my arm. I'd been lucky. Another night, and I would've died. That's what Dr. Remington told Vicky, making her cry. I felt as if I'd done something wrong and was too tired, too afraid to ask.

All the while Special Agent Martinez stood inside my room with another taller, older agent who hadn't introduced himself yet. Vicky had been pitching a fit since she'd been hauled out of the room so they could process me.

"He is my son," she hissed at Special Agent Martinez. "You have no right."

"Jordan Brooks belongs to the State of Montana. He's not your son." The first thing Special Agent Martinez said since he arrived almost an hour ago. The nice, tempered agent was gone and replaced by a stone-cold law enforcement officer with dark eyes. Vicky's expression hardened. The agent seemed to realize she was getting ready to attack and he sighed. "We have probable cause and a warrant, Ms. Manning."

"Are you charging him?"

He looked at me. "Not yet."

I looked from him, to her, back to him. "What's going on?" Vicky took my hand in hers and I pulled away hating the pained look on her face, but she didn't try to touch me again.

"Jordan," the taller agent said. He stood closer to my bed, his features grandfatherly with kind, brown eyes and his hair cut short and clean. "My name is Special Agent Luke Ferrell. I'm going to ask you some questions and I need you to answer them to the best of your abilities."

The IV insertion sight itched, and I scratched it. "May I have some water?"

Vicky quickly grabbed the large water container and served me some. "Do we have to do this now?" she asked.

"Dr. Remington cleared him for a few hours. It is best we get his version of events now, Ms. Manning."

Vicky turned her glare to Special Agent Martinez. "Do I need a lawyer?"

"He hasn't been charged," SA Ferrell said not unkindly.

"Charged for what?" I asked.

"Jordan," SA Ferrell said, drawing my attention back to him. "You were found with the body of Penny Cartwright. Can you tell me what happened?"

"She was already there when I fell," I said, staring at Special Agent Martinez who didn't look away. I couldn't read his expression. He looked like a stone statue, his features frozen. Like the dead. Though I knew he didn't believe me, and it scared me. *He* scared me.

"What time was that?"

"I don't know."

"Can you try to remember?" the agent asked, a little more forcibly. Special Agent Martinez remained silent, allowing SA Ferrell to lead the questioning.

"He says he doesn't know," Vicky said. "He's just suffered from hypothermia which causes confusion, as I'm sure you are well aware. Don't lead him to answer questions he's not comfortable with."

Wow, I wanted to hug Vicky at that moment. She could've been a lawyer.

"My apologies," SA Ferrell said and turned to me. "Jordan, do you know what happened to Penny?"

"No."

"Jordan, you disturbed the scene. I need to know exactly what you saw in that cave."

"I had no choice."

"I understand. Can you tell me what you saw?"

I did. I told him about the rug, the coat, the purse, and everything I took out of it.

"When was the last time you saw Penny?" SA Ferrell asked.

"I don't know what time. She was with Riley at Quinn's."

"Was she still there when you left?"

"I think so."

SA Ferrell looked at his notebook. "I'm trying to piece together a timeline, Jordan. Can you help me with that?"

No. I didn't want to help him with anything. "Sure," I said instead.

"If she was still at the house when you left—which according to witnesses pegged the time at about ten—and witnesses reported Penny leaving an hour after, how is it that you ended up in that cave after she'd already been placed there?"

I tore my eyes away from him and kept them on my hands. A slow burning pain of embarrassment rushed through me. Telling them I'd been locked in my trunk for hours and pissed myself felt worse than admitting to being a killer. Though I wasn't a killer. "Did you check Hector?"

"His car," Special Agent Martinez elaborated when SA Ferrell lifted a brow.

"Yes."

"And what did you find?"

"We found your keys in the ignition, your dead cell phone in the passenger seat along with the clothes you were wearing in the backseat." There was a slight pause. "They were soiled. The pants and the trunk. With urine."

Heat lifted up to my cheeks.

"Why don't you tell us what happened, Jordan?"

I couldn't, so I lied. "I don't remember."

"Do you remember walking through the woods near Pike's Pass?"

I closed my eyes. "I wasn't walking," I heard myself say as I turned onto my side, away from everyone in the room, and curled myself into a tight ball. "I was running away from the man chasing me." I couldn't say it'd been the sheriff because I hadn't seen him. They wouldn't believe me anyway. They'd never believe a loon. I just wanted them to go away. "I fell in the hole and then Dad called me. He promised me nothing would ever hurt me again, but he lied. He lied."

For a moment I thought I'd been left alone. The room was so silent. Maybe everything had been a dream.

"How did your dad call you, Jordan?" SA Ferrell asked.

"He called Penny's phone. I told him where I was. That's how you found me."

"Jordan, there is no father listed on your birth certificate. Do you know who he is?"

I heard Vicky get to her feet. "I think we're done here. He's confused and needs to rest."

I appreciated her at that moment more than she'd ever know.

I didn't do anything wrong. Okay, so maybe I failed to mention Steel shoving me into my trunk and pissing myself. Failed to mention the scar at my neck. But I wasn't a killer.

Don't be sure about that.

That quick thought rattled me.

"You'll be hearing from us if we have more questions," Special Agent Ferrell said before the room silenced.

Vicky let out a long breath. She'd doubt me too. I knew it. I let myself sleep and a few hours later opened my eyes to someone near my bed and the smell of peppermint and weed. I fell asleep again. Two days later, I was released from the hospital.

ELIZABETH ARROYO

Chapter Twenty-Four

The following days melded into a series of light and darkness. And cold rain turning to slushy snow. I watched the weather patterns outside my window while burrowed under my covers.

The nightmares started the night I'd been released from the hospital. They started with Penny angry at me for being dead and ended with me running from the mad man in the woods. Every time he caught me, I'd see Special Agent Nate Martinez before I woke up. I decided not to sleep so I watched the window.

Aimee had come to visit me on one of those days. She talked about how everyone had been so worried about me. The whole community came out to search the woods. It'd been sheer luck that Mrs. Brainard got lost along the cavern pass with her dog Moose. Mrs. Brainard had a horrible sense of direction. Aimee had chuckled at that truth.

I remained silent. Staring at the fractals of snow as it clung to the window for life before it melted away. At least Aimee didn't force me to get out of bed. She simply tapped my leg, planted a kiss on my temple, and walked out.

She didn't come back.

The following day, Riley did much of the same. Except that he just sat at the edge of my bed and stared out the window with me. While I contemplated my own broken mind, I was pretty sure he was contemplating Penny's death. He didn't have to tell me how he was probably the prime suspect. He'd been with Penny that night. I thought at one point of easing his mind and admitting to killing her just so he could be let off the hook.

But then I remembered, I hadn't killed her.

And someone normal wouldn't lie about killing someone. So I'd said nothing and he left too.

Mr. and Mrs. Harris had visited with food. Mr. Harris was too big to fit in the house, but he managed. Mrs. Harris and Vicky got to talking while Mr. Harris and I had snuck out to the backyard for a few minutes. We didn't even talk. His presence was enough to make me feel better.

The no door thing made it hard not to listen in on Vicky's arguments with the state social worker that came by to pick apart Vicky's life. The young woman knew Vicky, everyone knew Vicky, and finally just admitted that it'd be best that Vicky return me. I didn't hear the end of that conversation. Then she argued with Jack Johnson for being an ass and finally she'd had enough.

"Jordan," Vicky said. "You have to get up."

I didn't want to get up. I couldn't be sure I could get up. She shook me hard. "Come on. I'm not kidding. It's been four days and all you've done is get up to use the bathroom and eat. Sheriff Johnson and Special Agent Martinez are here to ask you questions."

By here, she meant inside my small bedroom, staring at me.

Growling, I shoved the blanket off myself, swung my legs over the bed and got to my feet. It took everything I had not to vomit. I waited a few seconds before moving, forcing them out of my bedroom.

The house was cold.

"We have more questions, Jordan," Sheriff Johnson said.

Special Agent Martinez leisurely looked around the house. Then he moved to the kitchen counter where I had left my journal. I knew he meant to peek inside, but I beat him to it and snatched it out of his hands. "That's private." I hugged the journal to my chest.

"My apologies," he said, but he didn't sound sorry.

"Vicky," Sheriff Johnson started the conversation this time. "We're here to get some answers about Penny. Jordan picked her up—"

"Yes, I was there. We have pictures."

Special Agent Martinez took a seat in front of Vicky. She had no choice but to look at him and shrink back with the death glare he was giving her. "The timeline of events does not match up, Ms. Manning. Either we get answers now or I charge Jordan Brooks with the murder of Penny Cartwright. We have more than enough forensic evidence to deduce as much. His prints are all over her."

"I had to move her to get the rug and coat," I argued in my defense. "I didn't do it."

Neither Sheriff Johnson nor Special Agent Nate Martinez reacted to my pitiful admission of innocence.

Vicky finally ran her hand through her hair. "Jordan, tell them what they want to know so they can leave us alone."

With that, she fed me to the wolves.

"What time did you arrive at the school?" Sheriff Johnson asked.

"Uh, early. I'd say about six. Mrs. Brainard was serving juice." He wrote it down in his notebook.

"When was the last time you saw her?"

"At Quinn's. The after party."

"With Riley Eaton?"

I felt as if I were throwing Riley under the bus. But I wasn't the only one to see him there with Penny. "Yeah, with Riley."

"Did you see them leave together?"

"No."

"What time did you leave the party?"

"I don't know. I didn't look at the time."

"Chase Cooper believes you left about ten thirty, but your car remained near Quinn's place. Jordan, I need you to think."

Chase had seen me walk off. He hadn't seen me leave because he left first. I didn't say any of that. Instead, I told them about getting locked in the trunk by Steel et al. I didn't mention the piss. They already knew.

"Those boys are nothing but trouble. They've been bullying him since he started high school and you've done nothing," she spat at Sheriff Jack Johnson.

"May I leave now?"

Sheriff nodded and I rushed into my room. Too bad I didn't have a door. I crawled back into my bed and threw the covers over myself, my head peeking out so that I could look out my window again. Two seconds later, I heard someone at the door.

When I didn't acknowledge him, he dragged my one chair near my bed, blocking my sight to the window so that I had to look at him and all his angry glory.

"And I thought you were the good guy," I snapped.

Special Agent Martinez arched a thick brow. "I'm not the good guy?"

"You think I killed her."

"Why would you say that?"

"Because you're being a dick."

He chuckled, his eyes crinkling with laughter. "Do you always say what's on your mind?"

"I don't lie, if that's what you're asking. And you already made me out to be guilty, so what do you want now?"

"You're right, Jordan. I get testy when I find

murdered innocents."

I looked away feeling guilty again for mentioning it. "She's still going to be dead," I grumbled.

"Excuse me?" he asked.

I caught his brown eyes. There was a layer of kindness there over all the ugly, it just wasn't for me. "When you find the killer. Penny will still be dead."

"I know. But maybe we can save the next one."

"So you think this is some sort of serial killer spree?"

He ignored my question with one of his own. "Jordan, you said someone was chasing you that night. That's how you fell in the hole."

"I don't know who it was. I didn't see his face. Only the truck. Do you believe me?" Hope surfaced and I wasn't sure why I wanted him to believe me. Apart from me ending up in jail, that is.

"We're looking into every possibility." He tapped his hand on his thigh. "We didn't find any unknown calls into Penny's phone like you said."

"Because I'm a loon. I don't even know my dad. He couldn't have called."

Special Agent Martinez looked away and tapped his notebook with the back of his pencil, his expression in stern concentration. There was something oddly soothing about that tap. Unlike Liam's hard taps, Special Agent Martinez's tap was softer. For some reason, I remembered the way he looked at the pictures of all those missing children.

"Have you ever lost anyone?" I asked.

I didn't think he'd answer, but he did. "Bellamy, my son. He would've been your age."

Bellamy. I liked the name. "How old was he when he died?"

"Six."

"My mother abandoned me when I was six."

His brow crinkled and it looked like he wanted to tell me something. He carefully unfolded a piece of paper and lifted it so I could see the drawing of three interlocking circles. The Borromean rings. "Can you tell me what this means to you?" he asked.

I lifted my eyes to his. "It means unity. Family." I'd give anything to be able to guard my expressions like Special Agent Martinez. There must've been an FBI class on how to control every muscle in your face so as not to give anything away.

"Can you tell me how you got that scar in the back of your neck?"

"Vicky said it was a birthmark." Not a lie.

"But you know it's not."

He got me there. "I don't remember."

"How did you know about Natalia's love of dolphins?"

"I looked her up on Instagram."

"Do you always look up clients?"

"Yes. I like giving the parlor a special personal touch the family might like. You can ask Mrs. Harris."

He nodded, folded the paper again, and put it in his pocket.

"I didn't kill her."

"I hope not. But we have to figure out who did."

"Riley wouldn't hurt her either."

"Who do you think would've hurt her?"

Jaylene. I didn't say the name. I remembered her trashed bedroom. The way she came at Penny at my locker. The way she looked at homecoming. She'd also been with Natalia before she was killed. And her words of world domination sounded too scary.

"Jordan?"

I blinked away the thoughts. "I don't know.

Maybe whoever killed Natalia."

"I have another question, Jordan. How well do you know the Coopers?"

That was a weird question. "I've been friends with Jaylene since third grade. I used to stay over at their house a lot."

He nodded. "Used to?"

"She wanted to upgrade me from friend to boyfriend, but I said no. She didn't like that, so…"

"So," he said. I liked him. He didn't lie or sugarcoat things. Didn't have to add false hope or anything. "If you remember anything else. You still have my number?"

"Yeah."

Sheriff Johnson tapped on the molding of the door. "We should head out," he said.

Special Agent Martinez rose to his feet. "Stay safe, Jordan," he said.

When they were gone, I got out of bed and met Vicky in the kitchen. I caught her wiping a tear on her face. I didn't ask about Sheriff Johnson. The thing must've been over. She turned around, anger pinched her features. "Tell me about your medication." She lifted the vial, opened it, and popped one in her mouth. "Cherry flavor. How original. I told you no lies."

"I told you I didn't want to take them anymore."

"You can't just stop. There are consequences!" I'd never seen her so angry.

I swallowed the lump in my throat. "Did you know they test those pills on rats! I'm not a rat!" I fisted my hands just to keep them from shaking.

Her face tightened and her lips pinched.

"Do you have any idea what happened to me when I was a kid?"

"No, Jordan. I do not. I wasn't *there.* I wasn't part

of your life, remember?"

"No, I don't remember. I don't remember anything! That's the point!"

"Go to your room. We'll talk later."

I charged into my bedroom and for the first time in my life I wished I had a door, so I could've slammed it.

Chapter Twenty-Five

I sat in Dr. Cooper's office bouncing my knee up and down in a nervous twitch as she waited for the answer to her question. "How are you doing?"

That's a loaded question if ever I heard one. People asked that all the time in passing as if not really expecting a real response. No one really cared how anyone was doing. They all wanted the answer to one question. Did I kill Penny Cartwright?

Something had unlatched in my mind. Like a wall had tumbled over a cliff and waters were flooding my brain. "Good," I lied.

"Ms. Manning mentioned you had stopped your medications some time ago."

I nodded.

"Why?"

"Because I wanted an erection," I answered. I could be truthful with that. She didn't smile or get red like Mr. Harris.

"Fair enough," she said. "It's for you to decide the quality of life you want to lead, Jordan. Some people do well with drugs, others with cognitive behavior therapy. Some with both. But we're a team. It means we should be working through these concerns together. Do you see me as part of your team?"

I hated when she spoke to me as if I were ten. "Yes," I said.

"Good. Any adverse effects with being off your medications? Are you experiencing anything that you'd like to talk about?"

I couldn't totally lie. She'd know it. "At first I felt as if I were dying. But after, I think I'm okay. I'm not like healed or anything. I still don't like doors."

"You hear the screams."

I nodded.

She got up slowly from her chair, something she always did, and walked to the open door. I didn't turn to see her close it, but I heard the snick as it closed. My heart rattled inside my chest and I had to concentrate on breathing. I stared out her windows, imagining I was anywhere else but inside this office. "How about now, Jordan. Do you hear the screams now?" she asked from inside the room.

"No," I answered.

"Can you look at me?"

I moved like molasses onto my feet. I turned to face her in front of the closed door. With a violent flinch, I pulled back until my ass hit the edge of her desk. I watched in horror as she opened the door and stepped out. Then she closed it. "I'm right here, Jordan. Can you hear my voice?"

You better answer or she's going to put you back on meds.

"Yes," I said.

"Can you open the door, Jordan? Can you follow my voice and open the door? Take one step. Just one."

I took a step.

She kept talking, her voice muffled.

"Can you touch the knob, Jordan? It's okay. I'm okay. Just right behind the door."

Don't do it, Jordan. Don't touch it. You know what's behind the door. It's a trick.

The room swayed, or I swayed I couldn't tell. It felt like I'd been doused in cold water. My chest rose and fell with every heavy breath. I'm fine. Her voice. Her voice is just beyond the door.

"Jordan?"

I could do this. I could. I just had to move.

I wasn't sure how many seconds, minutes, hours

I'd stood there. It felt like years when Dr. Cooper slowly opened the door. It wasn't until she stepped inside that I realized I'd somehow moved back against the desk, my hands clawing at the edge.

"You did good, Jordan. Look at me. Can you look at me?"

I dragged my eyes from the door to her face and she smiled. She had a nice smile that touched her eyes. "You did good."

Some of the tension melted off my body. I felt lightheaded, but whatever tether I had to the door faded. It was open now. Safe. "I didn't. I couldn't."

"But you didn't faint this time."

Right. All the other times I'd passed out like I did at the funeral home. I forced a smile on my face. "Yeah. Okay. Can I go now?"

We talked a little bit more. She wanted to start immersion therapy with me. Get me outside and facing other types of doors. Next month. I'd be okay next month. We didn't talk about Penny.

Vicky spoke to Dr. Cooper briefly and drove us back home. Once I got home, I pulled out my journal and flipped it to an empty page and started drawing circles. Interlaced. Rings that meant unity because we were a family. The memory jolted out of me in waves. I started to rock myself, something I hadn't done since I was a kid. I don't know how I remember, but I did. Rocking soothed me. It kept me moving. Generating energy without hurting myself or someone else. I rocked as I drew rings in my journal. Because family mattered. "Sage. Kale. Rosemary. Peppermint. Caper. My name is Basil." I kept repeating the names over and over because they were my family.

I just couldn't remember them.

Mrs. Lyle, my caseworker, came by the house to

talk to Vicky. Vicky had taken her outside for the conversation so I wouldn't hear what they were saying. I saw them through the window. Vicky cried. My heart felt broken.

I woke up to my stomach growling and my face pressed into my notebook. I'm sure I had rings on my face from the bleeding ink. It'd turned dark outside. I walked out of my room. Not much place to hide from Vicky. She was in the kitchen cooking breakfast. It made my stomach rumble. "Come eat when you're done," she said, not in an angry way.

I used the bathroom, washed my hands, and sat with her at our small table off the kitchen.

She got to her feet, poured herself a glass of wine, and returned to the table. I could tell by the haze in her eyes that she'd been drinking for a while. I ate silently. Then she cleared the plate and sat down. I couldn't look at her. The one thing she had asked of me—not to lie to her—the one thing I did, and I wasn't sorry for it.

She placed her hand on mine. Instinctively, I moved it away. I wanted to tell her it wasn't her. I just didn't like to be touched. I didn't.

"You're right. I don't know what happened to you before you came into the system. No one knows. Your mother left you with a babysitter and never came back. You were assigned to a caseworker who left on maternity leave three weeks after. Your case was handed from worker to worker. Jordan, only the minimal was done to try to find your family. But nothing turned up. Your records were vague. It was just you against the world." She sipped her wine. "I thought I could help you."

I sucked in air. She was returning me. She thought she failed so she was returning me. Desperation and panic burned into my belly. "Are you sending me back?"

Her lips parted and her eyes widened in shock.

She reached for me but stopped herself. "No, sweetie. Oh, God. No."

I let out a breath and some tears slipped out of my eyes, down my face. I wiped them quickly away.

"I just meant, I don't know if I'm helping or making things worse anymore." She took a sip of her wine and gently placed it on the black coaster I'd made for her in fifth grade. A drawing of her house, the blue color had faded into a light gray. "Wait here." She got up and walked to the guest bedroom which she'd turned into an office and came back with a box. She gently put it on the table. "This is what the police found in your mother's apartment after they found you. The state gave it to me for you. There's not much in there, but maybe you should take a look."

I didn't know what to say.

"Are you sure you want to do this?" she asked.

My voice croaked. "Yeah."

"Then go for it." She gave me a small smile. "I'm heading to the store. Do you want anything?" I knew she was just giving me some privacy and I really appreciated it.

"No. I'm okay."

She stood by the door and turned to me with sad eyes. "I love you, Jordan. You know that right?"

"I know," I said, feeling a little bit scared because that was a lie too.

"You'll always be my son."

I didn't know what she wanted me to say, so I didn't say anything.

She walked out. I didn't move for the box until I heard her drive off.

Not sure why I felt scared, I opened the box and pulled out a few photo albums. I ignored those. Vicky was right. There wasn't much. But what I did lock onto was the worn, dirty teddy bear sitting at the bottom of the box.

A ghost of my past.

Are you sure you want to do this?

I slowly picked it out of the box. Its once brown fur had turned a darker shade, but it was the same teddy bear I had as a child. I remembered feeling safe with it. The one thing that had come with me throughout everything.

It had survived and I with it.

I slowly grazed my fingers on the underside where I knew there was a hidden pocket. I felt the zipper teeth.

The answers are just inside. All I have to do is unzip it and pull it out.

I don't know how I knew that, but I did.

Headlights speared into the room launching me to my feet and giving me an excuse to avoid Teddy for now. I carefully put him sitting on the chair and peeked out through the window at the truck sitting in my driveway with Chase inside. The last time I'd seen Chase, he'd kissed me then pushed me away. But he *had* kissed me back. I hadn't imagined that part of it. And yet, something like anticipation fluttered through me. A minute passed and he hadn't moved, so I walked out. Dumb move. Only in thin PJs and fuzzy Yoda slippers, I shuddered at the cold. I heard the locks disengage and I sprinted toward the truck and climbed in.

The instant change in temperature made me shiver again and he turned up the heat. "You shouldn't be outside," he said. His features under the shadows looked sharp and angular, but when the light hit his eyes, they looked worn-out with dark rims.

"You shouldn't be creeping."

"I'm not creeping."

"Sitting inside your car for the past few minutes without moving is creeping."

"Do you want to go somewhere?"

I did. So bad. "Sure."

We parked near the football field at the school. Quiet this time of night on a weekday. The stars were bright. We didn't get out of the truck. Too cold. He pulled his letterman jacket from the back seat and wrapped it around my shoulders. It was stiff leather that smelled of him with his name embroidered in the back. I put my arms through the sleeves, realizing then how much bigger he was than me.

"Thanks," I mumbled.

"You know," he said after a while. "I was always jealous of what you had with Jaylene. You were both so perfect for each other. She was really happy with you. Things seemed normal when you were around. My parents always told me to stay away from you. They thought you were therapeutic for her, and I'd mess it up if I befriended you. And Jaylene isn't one to share." He chuckled, but it was dry and painful. "You probably know her better than anyone." He paused, watching the field. "Then you turned her down. She came home that afternoon in one of her moods. She'd torn everything of yours from the guest bedroom, and you saw her room. Dad threatened to commit her again if she didn't calm down. Then they blamed me, as if I were the reason for your decision." I swallowed the lump as he turned to look at me. "I didn't think I was the reason and then you said what you said at homecoming. Am I the reason you turned her down?"

My immediate response was yes. But the more I thought about it, the more I realized, it wasn't exactly Chase. "I'm gay," I said bluntly. "I don't like girls."

"But you like me?"

"I thought you liked me too. I'm sorry—"

He grabbed my hand. It startled me that I liked it so much. "Don't, Jordan," he said. "I'm so sorry. That kiss. I've wanted to kiss you for so long. I liked you for so long. I panicked. I didn't mean to hurt you. I went back, but you weren't there. Your car was there, and I looked for you at Quinn's, even drove to your house, but I couldn't find you. I figured you went home with Aimee. And then the cops showed up at my house saying you were missing. I went to our spot, the stream. I thought maybe since I hurt you, maybe you went somewhere. I didn't know what to think."

"What happened to me is not your fault."

"I pushed you away, Jordan. I hurt you."

I slid my hand away from his. "You don't have to be nice to me because you feel guilty. I won't tell anyone. We could go on ignoring each other." The words hurt so much but I'd rather distance myself from him than get hurt again. I didn't think I'd survive it a second time.

"Jesus, Jordan. Is that why you think I came to see you? Because I feel guilty?"

"Had I not gone missing would you be sharing this with me?"

He didn't answer, but he didn't have to. I shoved my hands under my thighs. "Can you please take me back home?"

He did. And before I hopped down from his truck, I heard him whisper, "I broke up with Tabby."

I couldn't stop because I knew I would want him to kiss me. I managed to open and close the door and watch him leave. It wasn't until I crumbled on my bed that I realized I was still wearing his jacket. And it smelled of peppermint and weed.

The same scent I'd caught in my hospital room.

Chapter Twenty-Six

The school vibrated with rumors of what happened to Penny Cartwright. People looked at me more than usual as I reached my locker. And it didn't get any better. Riley and Aimee were MIA throughout the day. Chase had ignored me all through first period and Liam was the only one to talk to me during gym.

Lunch was awkward. I scanned the hall for Aimee wanting to pick her brain about my memories. Aimee would know what it all meant. She knew all about the mind stuff and I didn't care if she used me for it so long as she gave me answers. I saw her at her corner with her girlfriends. Back to the spot she held before dating Riley. Away from the freak side of the lunchroom. Away from me. I didn't see Riley at all.

Liam came up next to me with his own tray of food, scanned the crowd, and said, "Follow me," as if we were on some kind of covert mission. Though not hiding very well. I felt the eyes on us like ice along my skin. He didn't even wait to see if I wanted to follow him at all. I actually did, but that was irrelevant.

We sat at one of the corner tables facing each other. "Have you seen Riley?" I asked.

He shook his milk as if it were chocolate milk and opened it. "No." He looked more constipated than usual.

"So," I started, unwrapping the sandwich flavor for today and taking a bite. "What do you want?"

"Why would I want anything?"

"Why are you sitting with me?"

"You don't want me to sit with you?"

I remembered the party before everything had gone to shit. I remembered him wanting to kiss me before he set me on a path to Chase. But he'd been drunk. Not sure if that counted as him liking me or just using me. And he did send me to Chase who found me repulsive. Or, at least repulsive that night. My almost dying jolted him into guilt-love, or guilt-like. Chase didn't love me. Was that a thing?

I almost forgot Liam was there until he angrily tossed his sandwich on his tray and got to his feet. "Whatever."

I panicked and stopped him, putting my hand on his tray. "Please. Stay. Beats being alone."

He rolled his eyes almost to the back of his head. "Wow, what a nice thing to say." He sat back down. It took him two seconds to get to why he sat with me. "I heard the cops asked you some questions about Penny. Did they mention anything?"

I threw normal out the window. "Why are you so nervous? Are you afraid you're next?"

He narrowed his bright blue eyes at me and leaned forward too. "Yeah, maybe."

I meant that as a joke. "Why?"

He rubbed the back of his neck. "Meet me after school." He got up taking his tray with him before I could respond.

That was the weirdest conversation in the history of conversations, and I still waited for him after school. Although he hadn't given me specific instructions as to where I should meet him. I sat inside Vicky's car. Hector was still with the police. I watched for Liam as the school's lot emptied out with only a few cars left including Riley's navy-blue Toyota and Finn's truck. I hopped out of the car and circled the school toward the field where a crowd of people gathered around Riley and Finn.

"Come on, do something. I know you and that

crazy piece of shit killed her," Finn said, shoving Riley who looked about ready to fold and spill all the secrets he didn't have.

I've never been much of a fighter. I'm still not. But something inside of me boiled over and I sprinted toward Finn without stopping.

Okay, so maybe blitzing an unsuspecting jock was nothing like the movies made it out to be. Slamming into Finn felt like slamming into a tree. I almost bounced back but he grabbed me by my waist and pummeled me to the floor. The crowd went wild.

I couldn't breathe. I broke something for sure.

Finn laughed and spat at me. "Look who came to help you. You're *girlfriend*." Then Finn sneered at me as I fumbled to my feet. "I don't have to be nice to you anymore. My dad dumped Vicky because of *you*. We all told her she should've given you up to the loony bin where you belong."

I wish I could say that anger propelled me with fifty times my weight and I beat the living daylights out of Finn Johnson. But I didn't. Mrs. Brainard stopped the fight, having heard the chaos. Everyone scurried like rats as she called our names. I ran behind Riley to his car. Everyone else crammed into unseen nooks and crannies.

"Hey," I called Riley, who ignored me. "Riley."

He stopped and turned to me wearing an expression I'd never seen on him before. Half crying but more pissed. He shoved me back. "I don't need your fucking help!"

I couldn't move. "Riley, I'm on your side."

He pointed a finger at my face. "Fuck you. Don't ever talk to me again."

I watched as he climbed into his car and sped off.

Riley. My friend.

The laughter behind me brought me face to face

with Jaylene. The look in her eyes rabid. That's the only way I could've described it. She gently rubbed my cheek with her warm hands. I heard bells, as if the heavens had spread open and were calling me. But I didn't believe in heaven.

"Poor baby," she said. "I told you this is the way things would go. I warned you that they wouldn't understand us."

"What did you do, Jaylene?" The words tumbled out of my mouth.

Jaylene didn't flinch. She didn't question. She didn't look appalled that I could suspect her. She smiled and leaned into me. Her lips grazed the shell of my ear, and instead of saying something, she kissed me before pulling back wearing that same smile.

Finn watched us suspiciously but melted when she got to him and whispered something to him that made him laugh. Yeah, *the thing* was going good for him. I wondered if anything between us had been real, or had she just been manipulating me like she was now doing to Finn.

My phone buzzed and I pulled it out of my pocket. I sneered at the number and answered. "I thought we were meeting after school."

"Yeah, at my place," Liam said as if I were an idiot.

I *was* an idiot. "I'm on my way."

Liam's ranch was a ten-acre lot with horses and rescue animals of all different kinds. Some awaiting entry into zoos or other wildlife preserves. I knew next to nothing about Liam. He was in twelfth grade but older than Chase. He'd failed a school year. He knew Natalia Montenegro and Special Agent Martinez by association. He had beautiful blue eyes and wanted to kiss me. Which had been a lie. And he also threw me to the wolves, aka

Chase. Practically told me Chase liked me when that had been a lie too.

By the time I reached his place, that was all I could think about. His lies. The bullying. My broken brain. The medications. And now Riley hated me, and Aimee turned back to being a snob. And I was meeting Liam *fucking* Grant because he ordered me to.

Angry didn't justify how I *felt*.

This writhing swirl of emotions inside of me was volcanic. A burp before the eruption. The gas before the toxic fuel splurged to the surface. Yeah, I was full of gas right now. It wasn't until I reached his living room and saw his handsome face that I felt the subtle bubble surrounding my putrefied emotions push out.

Then he whistled as if I were a dog and said, "Come here, Basil."

Basil.

Not Jordan.

That bubble burst and I lunged on him like a baby monkey with a mission.

"What the fu—" That's as far as he got when he fell onto the sofa letting out a whoosh of air from his lungs as I landed on top of him.

I didn't let go, straddling him, hanging onto his head with both hands as if he were a coconut and I was trying to determine how much liquid was inside. Well, Liam wasn't a coconut and shaking his head didn't bode well for me. He fought me. I tried to turn his head to get a better look at the back of his neck. He called me Basil, which meant he knew. He knew. He was a part of whatever the branding meant. But he buckled, lifting me off him for a fraction of a second before he slammed me back against the sofa.

"Jordan, are you fucking crazy!" Yeah. Yeah. I was but I wasn't letting it out yet. I bit my lip hard to keep from mumbling my own curse words. We were two mammals fighting for dominance. Finally, he seemed to call it and grabbed my wrist pinning them at my sides, his body on me. Okay, so he was bigger than me. Everyone was bigger than me. "What is wrong with you?"

"Basil!" I yelled. "Why did you call me Basil?"

"I wasn't calling *you* Basil. I was calling the dog!" The veins on his forehead bulged, his face red and flushed with all kinds of angriness until he realized something. Then I realized something when I realized he realized the same thing. "Basil?" He said it so softly, so heartachingly familiar that I found myself boneless under him. Then the space between his eyes folded, his nostrils flared. He pressed his elbow and forearm against my stomach, and I couldn't breathe or move. Then he used his free hand to turn my head, searching out the same thing I had been searching on him.

The brand.

Ignoring my useless slaps, his fingers grazed the back of my neck, parted the hair, and then—

"What the hell?"

As if burned, Liam jumped off me. I couldn't see the owner of the voice, but I didn't have to. Liam looked genuinely frazzled. Hands shaking, eyes bulging, breathing hard. His hair and clothes rumpled. "Chase, what are you doing here?" he asked.

"The jump drive, *moron*. I told you I needed the demo."

"Right." Liam masked whatever the hell he'd been feeling with a smile, pointed two fingers at Chase and winked. "I'll be back." And then he sprinted out of the living room.

I took that moment to breathe. Maybe to try and hide. If volcanic eruptions *could* hide. The back of the sofa was a safe divider between Chase and me.

"I know you're there, *Jordan*," he said.

I sat up, fixing my shirt. It had lifted during the altercation with Liam. "Hey," I said, as if I were just chilling. With limbs shaking from the exertion, I got to my feet.

Chase glared at me. I'd never seen him so angry. Not even with Jaylene. "Nice to know you moved on so fast."

I started to plop my hair down but stopped. "Moved where?"

Chase rolled his eyes. He did that a lot when I was around. "Stop fucking pretending. You know exactly what I mean."

Oh, God. This was a normal test thing, and I was failing. I kept my mouth shut. Better to not say anything than to incriminate myself. But he narrowed the gap between us as if ready to bowl me over. I hit the back of the sofa and put my hand on his chest just to stop him from shoving me back into the sofa. I didn't think I could handle another wrestling match. Not with Chase. Not the way I wanted other things with Chase even though I should've been mad at him for hurting my feelings. But then I had practically forced that kiss on him. He hadn't wanted to kiss me. He had every right to shove me back and hate me. So why was he angry and so damn close to me now? Why did his eyes lower to my lips and then back to my eyes? Why was his heart pounding so hard against my palm as if he'd finished a game?

"You kissed me and now you're with *him*?"

Him who? I had to process his words for a second longer just to wrap my head around what he was *actually* saying. Then it hit me like a freight train. Chase was jealous. He thought I was with Liam. Like *with* Liam. "You pushed me away."

"You blitzed me."

"You kissed me back." I remembered that part. "You *liked* it." I added salt to the wound.

He grinded his molars. I could see his jaw bunching up. "Are you with him now?"

"No." I didn't need further explanation of what he meant.

"Do you want to be with *me*?" His eyes took in my face as if he were cataloguing me in his mind. Putting me into a database. As if he were trying to read every muscle movement I couldn't make. Then his eyes met mine and didn't turn away.

"Yes," I said on an exhale.

His warm hands cradled my face. Closer than we'd ever been, even when I first attacked him. Every inch of our body touching and then he—

—took a step back.

"Got it," Liam said, holding out a stupid jump drive.

Chase snatched it from his fingers, spun on his heels, and walked out as silently as he had arrived.

"You're welcome!" Liam called behind him, then he turned to me, pretty much with my mouth open, probably drooling. No, not drooling. Please, not drooling. Chase liked me. He had been about to kiss me. I hadn't imagined that. The warm fuzzies scattered into the wind when Liam spoke. "So, Basil. I thought you were dead."

Chapter Twenty-Seven

"Stop staring at me," I growled for the hundredth time since Liam dragged me to his bedroom and sat me at his desk to go over my past.

Liam paced. "I can't help it, dude." He shook his head. "I remember you as this tiny thing who used to sleep on my arm with that dirty ass teddy bear you never let go." More head shaking. "And you're here. Alive. I heard you died. *Died.*"

"Yeah, I got that part," I mumbled.

He went on to say what other things he remembered when I didn't remember anything but the falling asleep in his arms bit. Kale. Liam was Kale. The boy who shared the cage with me. The boy *The Parents* threatened to put behind the door if I didn't come back. That had been how they controlled us. According to what Liam had dug up over the years, I'd been the youngest when they were caught. There wasn't much he could tell me, and our names were kept confidential so I couldn't find much online.

Joseph and Maureen Bateman were serial killers who terrorized the state, killing six women and four minors before they were caught. The Batemans used children to lure their victims.

I'd already thrown up twice reading this and every time my eyes glossed over the words, I felt sick again. The picture of a boy whose body was found in an unmarked grave seven years after he'd been abducted from his Montana home stared back at me from the screen. Underneath the image of the then seven-year-old boy read that he'd been the child of Rufus and Abigail Harris. Matthew had been thirteen at the time of death.

The oldest of us.

Sage.

Harris.

I knew his family. They felt like my family. By that point, everything inside me hurt.

"I don't remember," I whispered.

"Maybe that's a good thing," Liam said, finally plopping down on his bed and staring at the ceiling. "The shit was awful. You were the youngest. Sage was the oldest and longest with them."

"What happened to him?" I whispered.

"They took him behind the door when they couldn't find you."

"You're the one that has to save them, Basil."

Them. He'd said them, not us. "He knew he was going to die the moment he put me in that grave."

Liam didn't say anything.

I took in his room for the first time since he dragged me up here. It was big, but simple. He had no posters on the walls, no musical instruments, the bed was bare, and the nightstand filled with little vial of medications. Like me, Liam was haunted too. But unlike me, he knew why.

I dragged my eyes away from him on the bed, ignoring this nudging feeling to lay down with him. I picked up the autobiography written by Dakota Simmons talking about how he survived the Bateman couple. The book that outlined every detail of the six children kidnapped by them. He didn't call us out by name, the law protected us as minors, but he had described us perfectly. All it cost him was his life. Caper died six months ago, six weeks after his book was released into the world. The tome felt heavy in my hand. As if all our souls were trapped inside.

We had been used to kill people. The screams

behind the door had been real. Six adults. Four kids. And I couldn't even remember their faces. *Maybe that's a good thing.*

"Do you think someone is trying to kill us?"

"Don't you? Caper is dead. Found in a riverbed in Nebraska. Natalia found around here, and I don't know who Peppermint really was, but I'm sure she's dead too. He ousted us. Put targets on our head. You and I are the only ones left."

"I don't remember Penny, do you?"

Liam's hands played with a pencil he'd plucked off the side table. Pencils were his thing. It calmed him to have something to do with his hands. Then I remembered the smaller version of his hands sifting through my hair whenever we were caged, his hands always fiddling with my clothes, making sure I was clean, touching me. Liam needed a connection with something, and he found a pencil. "No," he said. "But she may have been a mistake or something."

I rolled my eyes. "That's a far reach, Liam." I got to my feet already feeling the need to run out of there. I couldn't do this. I couldn't. This was all wrong. "I have to go." I rushed out of the room.

Liam followed me. "Jordan, wait. There's more you have to remember."

"No. I can't. I can't do this right now." My brain felt like it was really going to burst. "Call me later." I ran out and got into my car. Hector got me out of there before I could puke some more. I realized I still had Dakota's book in my hand.

I drove without thinking. I just wanted everything out of my head. I didn't want to remember. I found myself passing Chase's house. His truck was the only car in the driveway. I parked behind him and headed to the front door.

What would Chase do if he found out his whole life was a lie? None of this was *normal*.

Chase flung the door open, and his smile turned into a frown fast. "I thought you were the pizza guy."

Okay, not what I expected. "Are you alone?"

"Yeah. Are you okay?"

"No. Can I come in?" I wasn't sure if I'd cry if he said no, but he opened the door wider and closed it behind me.

I knew this house like I knew my own. It was so quiet when it was empty, except for the music floating down from Chase's bedroom. It was the only time he could listen to his music the way he wanted. The only time he wore that smile. I didn't wait for the question or invitation, I headed to his bedroom which thankfully was open and empty. I didn't think I could survive a closed door right now.

I heard him behind me. "Jordan, you're freaking me out here."

Finding some courage way deep inside of me, I turned to face him. He'd showered, the tips of his hair wet, and his face clean. No liner. He wore a white t-shirt and PJ bottoms with emoji's on them and his feet were bare. I took him in slowly. I wanted this moment to last in my memory. Forever. I'd never felt so exposed in my life. But I was done with feeling incomplete. Broken. His blue eyes held mine and his breathing picked up. Now or never. "Do you like me?" My pulse drummed in my ears as the words made space between us. I couldn't take them back. I didn't want to take them back.

He didn't move. Didn't say anything. He waited like a stone statue. The silence made me realize what a mistake I'd just made. He didn't care about me. Not at all. But then—

—the doorbell rang.

"Pizza," he whispered out as if he'd been jogging a mile. Then he turned and rushed out.

Pizza.

Saved by the pizza man.

I felt sick. Clarity returned in waves of desperation. I sprinted down the stairs and outside just as Chase was paying for the pizza. I didn't stop when he called my name. I jumped in my car like the coward that I was because anything was better than facing the rejection of Chase Cooper.

Do you like me? Did I really think that Chase Cooper could like me? That moment in his truck had been him feeling guilty because *I* had kissed *him* and he'd pushed me away. And yet, a big part of me wanted to believe it could be true. And I wanted to smack myself for it.

I drove to the only place where I didn't feel like such a mess. The place where I felt I belonged.

Mrs. Harris opened the door for me, and I couldn't help but to see how much Sage looked like her. Guilt rushed over me at not making the connection sooner. Sage had been a shape in my head. I had filled the rest of him in my mind when I couldn't remember him. All this time, he'd been here in this very room, among the pictures on the wall, on the mantel, and inside the broken pieces of Mr. and Mrs. Harris. Good people who hadn't deserved to lose their son.

I should've told them how Sage saved us. I should've told them how he was the bravest person I'd ever known. But I didn't want to lose them. I needed them more than Sage right now, so I shoved my hands into my coat pocket and kicked at the snow at my feet. "I'm sorry to barge in. I was wondering if I can help with something." Being busy here was better than being in my mind alone.

"Oh, sweetie," she said kindly and hugged me. I usually didn't like hugs or touches, but hers felt familiar. "You don't need an excuse to visit." She pulled away from me and opened the door wider, and it felt like home. "Mr. Harris is in the garage if you'd like to make sure he's still breathing."

Mr. Harris had a lot of projects he was working on. The last one had been reupholstering an old armchair he found in a yard sale. It'd taken him ten days and seven stitches on his hand before he finished that one. Mr. Harris with a staple gun was dangerous business.

The garage was warm, having its own heater. Mr. Harris couldn't even blend in with the shadows. The guy was so big. I felt safe with him. The same way I had felt with Sage. With Matthew. His dead son. Died saving us. Saving me. I'd never had a dad, never wanted to connect with anyone, until now.

"Hey Jordan," he said, stopping his range of motion and looking at me wide-eyed. I felt guilty making them worry. I felt guilty not being able to tell them the truth. Afraid of losing them and turning up on some killer's list.

"Sorry. I should've called when I felt better."

Mr. Harris cleared his throat. He wasn't a mushy type of man and kept his feelings in check. I liked that about him. "Thought I'd get this done before the winter really gets here."

"Do you need help?"

"Sure, get me the clamps." He pointed and I followed his instructions. Mr. Harris was a patient man with a voice that should be on late night radio. Once we settled into a rhythm together, we didn't need conversation. Another thing I liked about Mr. Harris. Being around each other was enough.

It wasn't until he was ready to call it quits that he

lifted dark eyes to me. "Everything okay, son?"

No. My whole life has been a lie. I knew your son before he died. I wish I was as brave as him.

I shrugged. Words were useless in this scenario.

He patted my shoulder. We ate dinner. I listened as they talked about the upcoming holidays. Vicky and I usually celebrated Thanksgiving with the Johnsons or just us. Vicky didn't have family, or at least I didn't think she did. We never visited and she never talked about them. I didn't ask. I was included in the Harrises' conversation with *What do you think, Jordan?* and *Have you ever tried it? Well, I'm going to have to make that for you, then.* By the time I walked out, I had a full belly, leftovers for Vicky, and I felt better.

Vicky had been using a rental to drive around and it wasn't in the driveway when I got home. A different car sat in my driveway. Not a car. A truck I immediately recognized. I pulled up beside it and got out at the exact same time Chase got out.

It was cold out. Snow already tempted the air.

I walked around my car, and he met me at my front door. He looked drained. As if he'd been crying. I wasn't sure if I should open the door, or what to say. I had no words left for him.

Apparently, he didn't either because he slowly cupped my face and leaned in to kiss me, giving me enough time to tell him to stop. I didn't tell him to stop.

Soft, cool lips gently suckled my bottom lip. I couldn't move. His lids slowly lifted as he pulled away and I couldn't even blink. My heart slamming against my ribcage made this real. The cold air pressed against my exposed skin made this real. Silence stretched between us and he didn't run, didn't shove me.

He kissed me!

Then he slanted his lips on mine again for another

kiss. This one deeper, sending all kinds of sizzling energy through me. My body turned pliant. I closed my eyes. Tears stung my cheeks. I didn't even know why I was crying. He did that thing again with my bottom lip and I followed his every movement. Even wrapped my arms around his neck to get closer. Our bodies pressed together. The kiss turned into a desperate thing as if pulling away meant instant death. And after the initial onslaught of tongue and teeth, it turned softer. I felt his hands on my face shake slightly as if he too was nervous. Or cold.

We pulled away, our foreheads leaning against each other, our breaths mingled between us. "Would you like to come inside?"

"Yes," he said. "I would."

Chapter Twenty-Eight

I woke up to Chase burrowed against my back, his arm around my waist, his breath tickled the back of my neck. I also felt all the messy left-over from last night.

Last night!

I remembered the kisses. The touching. The more kisses and more touching. I laced our fingers together. He shifted, breaking slowly from sleep. His breathing deepened. Then he moved closer. His chest flushed against my back. His morning wood pressed against my backside because we were still naked.

Naked!

"Don't freak out," he mumbled in the sexy husky voice I had imagined in my dreams.

"I'm not going to freak out," I said. Totally about to freak out.

"Your heart just started to speed up. That means you're about to freak out."

"Should I freak out?"

He burrowed his face deeper into my neck. "No. This is good. We're good."

"But-but it's already morning. What if your parents reported you missing?"

He chuckled as if that were not possible. "They won't. They don't care about me."

That hurt my soul for some reason.

"They're not overbearing assholes, just assholes," he clarified.

"Oh." Not sure if that was better.

The silence stretched on too long and I thought I should be responsible and not let him fall asleep again. "We have to get ready for school," I whispered. Already morning, Vicky should've gone to work. But then if she came in last night, saw Chase's truck, and then peeked into my room—

Yeah, I was in so much trouble.

"It's Saturday," he said. "And it's fucking cold in here." He shivered behind me. "We should bail and go get some breakfast."

I heard Vicky in the kitchen. Having no door suddenly sucked. "Uh, Vicky might have other ideas."

He let out a long sigh I felt flutter down my spine. "Right," he said. "The Parent."

I stiffened at the mention of The Parent. The visual I had wasn't of soft smiles and warmth. It was cold and the door. The screams and the blood.

"Hey," Chase said, getting up on his elbow to look at my face, sensing my rise to panic. "I'm sure we can come up with a story. I have friends over all the time." The concern in his expression for me pushed the terrible thoughts away. "We can keep this between you and me, if you want."

He mistakenly thought my current state of panic had to do with us and I nodded like an idiot without correcting him. "I want. Yeah." I couldn't think with him so close.

Something like disappointment flashed across his expression. I knew that look. Saw it on Vicky whenever I did something wrong. He quickly looked away from me and started to pick his clothes from the floor. "No, you're right." He sounded as if he were trying to convince himself. "I should go home."

I held onto the sheet as if he were going to tear it away, exposing me raw. "Okay."

He didn't look at me as he dressed, shoved his feet into his boots, grabbed his coat, and silently walked out. I heard him greet Vicky before the door opened and closed. I knew she hadn't moved from the kitchen.

"You can come out now," she called.

Shit. She knew.

I let my body go lax on the bed, wishing for the folds of the lumpy mattress to bury me. I still felt Chase all around me as if he hadn't really left at all. Part of him still lingered and I wanted to hold on to it. I should've said something, like don't leave. Or sure, I'd like to be your boyfriend. Right. He hadn't asked. He'd just given me what I had asked of him. A kiss that led to something more. That made me forget for a few hours that my whole life had been a lie. I thought that would've made me feel better, but I still woke up to the glaring lie. Only now, I had another lie wedged into my heart.

Chase.

I couldn't consolidate how I felt for him. What I felt for him. What he felt for me.

My head was fuzzy. A mess.

Not right.

Reluctantly, I got out of bed and dressed. I tried to look presentable before I met Vicky in the kitchen. I sat on one of the two stools at the counter and stared at the ugly laminate countertop. We didn't have many nice things, but at least we had something.

"So," she said using her soft voice. "Chase Cooper, huh?" I heard a slight smile in her voice and lifted my eyes to her. Vicky had always been Vicky. She wore a crooked smile and watched me as if waiting for me to freak out. I wondered if this was an appropriate time to freak out. Instead, I felt my cheeks heat up.

"I, uh, like him."

She drummed her fingers close to my hand. She wouldn't touch me unless I precipitated the touch first. And I did. I brushed my fingers along hers. "It's okay if you're gay, bi, straight, queer, pan, curious or anything else I forgot."

I smirked. "You just looked that up."

She shrugged one shoulder. "Thought I should be prepared to give you some advice." She leaned forward, resting on her elbows. "Be safe, Jordan. Condoms are a thing."

I rolled my eyes and had to get out of there before I exploded in rainbow-colored confetti. "Yes, *Mom*," I said dryly.

She took in a sharp inhalation of breath. "What did you say?"

"I said, yes…" *Mom*. "Mom," I said slowly. I called her *Mom*.

She moved around the counter and wrapped me in a bear hug that didn't freak me out. "There's hope for us yet." I liked that she said *us*. It felt like *us*. She kissed the top of my head.

I didn't squirm away. It actually felt nice.

"So what are your plans for this weekend?"

"I'd like to spend it with Chase, but I think I upset him."

We sat on the sofa. "How?"

"I told him I wanted to keep us a secret." Vicky made a face as if she totally understood why Chase would be upset while I had no clue. "I just don't want to ruin it. If people found out, they'll tell him things about me."

"What things?"

Like I helped kill people. I felt sick.

"Jordan?"

Thankfully, someone knocked on the door before I could vomit. Vicky gave me that look that we weren't done and opened the door. Special Agent Nate Martinez stood in the doorway, and I got to my feet, hoping that he'd caught and charged someone for Penny.

"Ms. Manning, Jordan, may I come in?"

Vicky didn't want to let him in, but she did anyway.

"I brought Hector. He's been cleaned and fixed. You should be safe to drive it now."

My lips parted, unhinged. "Uh, thank you."

"And?" Vicky asked.

"Except for Penny's prints in the passenger side which was a result of her being in your car, we don't have enough evidence to charge Jordan."

Vicky tsked as if she knew all along. It made me feel a lot better. Though not really because Special Agent Martinez had still looked for evidence to charge me. It meant he thought I could kill someone. That made me feel bad for some reason.

"I'm heading back to New York for a while. If you need anything, please reach out to me." He handed Vicky his card and me another one.

For some weird reason, I didn't want him to go to New York. I wanted him to stay here and find Penny's killer. "What about the case?" I asked.

"Sheriff Johnson has a team."

Vicky scoffed. Though I knew it had more to do with her heart, than his skill of catching killers. "Have they released her body?"

"Yes."

"Is her murder linked with Natalia's?" I held my breath.

"I can't divulge that information. Do you think they are related?" he asked, the space between his brow folded.

I felt Vicky's hand on my forearm. "We'll call if we have anything else," she said.

He nodded but didn't move away. "May we speak?" he asked Vicky. "In private?"

I felt her hand shake on my arm and I wanted to fling myself between them and protect her. But she nodded curtly and grabbed her jacket. "Be safe Jordan,"

Special Agent Martinez said to me and waited for Vicky near his car.

They were too far to hear. Vicky kept her eyes lowered, kicking at the snow at her feet as Special Agent Martinez talked. He said something that made her angry and she shoved a pointed finger at his chest.

"Just leave him be." I heard Vicky say clear enough.

Special Agent Martinez shook his head. No. He wasn't going to let *him* be. Whoever the *him* was in this conversation.

You, Jordan. The him *is you.*

I rubbed my sternum because it hurt in a spot just behind my ribs.

Vicky wiped her face, turned around, and stalked back to the house.

I ducked into my room and watched as Special Agent Martinez beat up his steering wheel before he took off.

I heard the door close, footsteps to my room, and I jumped on my bed in time to avoid being caught snooping. Vicky's eyes were glazed with tears. "What aren't you telling me, Jordan?"

I was so screwed.

Chapter Twenty-Nine

First period had been awkward. Chase acted like his usual self and only sent me a small smile of hello when I watched him swagger inside the classroom. Then at lunch he'd been with his regular friends—his bandmates and Tabatha. Though they weren't sitting close together. She did look like a mess and eventually, they walked out together. I didn't know what that meant and almost followed them just to be a stalker, but Liam took that moment to charge toward me, and Chase fizzled out.

"We need to talk." Liam had a cute angry face too. I tried to merge this version with the younger version I barely remembered but couldn't.

"Can I eat?"

He grabbed my wrapped sandwich and shoved it into his pocket and did the same with the milk and orange. Then he grabbed my tray and dumped it before glaring at me as if warning me to say no. I followed him out of the lunchroom and to the library where we signed out an available study room.

Once we were alone, he unpacked my food from his pockets, and I ate as he paced.

He finally plopped down on the chair in front of me like a little whirlwind deflating. "I've been calling you."

"I know. You called me six times. I was ignoring you."

He narrowed his eyes at me, lips pressed together. "I've been thinking," he started, and I almost said, uh, oh. "Penny is the only one that doesn't fit."

"So maybe it's a different killer." I took a bite of

my sandwich. It was pretty good.

Liam glared at me. "How could you just eat at a time like this? We are targets. *Targets* and you're eating?" I ignored his rant. I was hungry. And I ate whenever I was nervous. I wasn't going to tell him that either. "Did you at least read the book?"

I had read it after I told Vicky about my scar and link to Natalia. I didn't tell her anything else. She said she had to think about things and left it at that. "Yeah." I wrapped the leftover sandwich, drank my milk, and put everything in a nice, neat bundle ready to trash.

Liam snorted, scooped everything up and tossed it into the garbage can in the room. I opened my mouth to tell him that wasn't for food but the way he was already glaring at me, I thought it safer to keep quiet.

Liam's expression dropped from sheer panic to incredulous and he sat down on the chair in front of me. "What do you know about Nate Martinez?"

I shrugged. "Nothing. He thinks I killed Penny."

Liam cocked his head. "And?"

"And that's it."

"You didn't tell him about—" He pointed to the general area of my neck.

"He knows. He saw it at the hospital when they processed me."

Liam swallowed hard. "Did he mention anything else?"

"He linked me with Natalia. I mean, he didn't say it right out, but he asked questions. Why?"

"I think he's Basil's father," Liam said slowly as if I wasn't Basil. As if Basil was someone else, someone whose past had been full of torture and fear. Not me. "The one mentioned in the book," he went on. "The one the police contacted first because it was his information in Basil's teddy bear."

I regretted eating because now it felt like a lump of coal burning forever in my belly.

He placed his warm hand on top of mine. For a moment it felt tingling, and I pulled my hand away. "Why would you think that?"

Liam started fiddling with his fingers. I almost wished he had a pencil instead. "After Natalia was found, he checked up on me. He knows I'm Kale."

"I told Vicky," I blurted, hoping to steer the conversation somewhere else.

It worked.

Liam remained so still I thought he turned to stone. His eyes glazed over with that familiar look I'd seen on Jaylene when she'd get lost in her head. I swallowed the lump in my throat wondering if I'd be able to pull him back into this reality, so I kept talking. "She asked me, and I didn't want to lie to her. I told her about the scar only. She said she has to think about what to do next."

He blinked out of the haze, and I let out a little relieved breath. "You *told* her?" He asked as if he hadn't just heard what I said. The accusation was there front and center.

Angry, I got to my feet. "I told her about *me*. Not you. Don't worry. You're safe." Liam stared at me, and I felt weird. Too weird. "I gotta go." I walked out. A bit of me wanted him to call me back. To tell me not to leave. To maybe come up with a plan that would keep us safe. But he hadn't.

I meant to go back into the hallway and go to class, but a soft sound of a bell had me walking in a different direction like a fly caught in light. The sound pulled me into my headspace. A safe place. Because at that moment all the hairs on my body stood on end and I realized instantly why. Fear. I was afraid.

The memory the chimes pulled from my head was Penny with the bracelet. The soft chimes of bells as she waved at her mom the night I took her out and promised to bring her back. Instead, she died. That image blurred to one of Jaylene after Riley had ended our friendship. Jaylene's nefarious smile, her cold eyes, and the soft touch of her fingers against my face. Caressing and mocking me at the same time because only Jaylene could make me feel worthy and guilty at the same time. And the soft chime of bells as her finger trailed my face. Penny's bracelet. Jaylene had been wearing Penny's bracelet.

I rounded the corner and caught the source of the chime. A computer. The soft sound of birds and bells floated from the speakers. Low and soothing. Except I felt nothing but a cold fear.

The rest of the school day went by in a buzz of jaded thoughts. Jaylene with Penny's bracelet. The feeling of needing to protect Liam. Wondering what Sage would think of me. He'd died for us. What would he think about me now? The coward? An innocent girl was dead, and I couldn't help but to think it was all my fault. And let's not forget the great big elephant in the room. My dad who thought I could kill someone. Special Agent Martinez knew about my scar. Did he know I was his son? Was I his son? And if I was his son, why did he leave me? Liam was right. I needed to know the truth, but first…I lifted my eyes and scanned the parking lot.

I caught Chase walking to his truck. I wasn't sure if he liked me anymore. I had hurt his feelings after we did what we did, and I hadn't been able to talk to him about it. I swallowed the lump in my throat and hated the way my voice sounded when I finally reached him. "Chase," I called. He turned around and after a moment of startled silence, he smiled. My heart gave a lurch in my chest, and I almost forgot what I'd meant to say. "I think there's something wrong with Jaylene," I blurted.

Wrong thing to say. His smile fell, replaced by a scowl. Chase narrowed the gap between us. "Really? You have to do this here?"

I swallowed the huge lump in my throat. "I think Jaylene was with Penny the night she died."

Chase grabbed my arm hard and dragged me away from the crowd forming in the parking lot. "What the fuck, Jordan? Why would you think that?"

"She told me."

"She told you she was with Penny."

"No, not in those words." He exhaled, losing his patience with me and I needed him to believe me so I rushed on, trying to put my thoughts into words that made sense. "You saw her bedroom. She attacked Penny at school. She's been acting differently. Listen, I know what I feel."

I'd said something wrong. The hard note of his words formed a knot in my stomach. "What you feel for my sister."

That was not a question, but it felt off. I opened my mouth to ask him to clarify, but he beat me to it and his words rushed through me. "Make up your mind, Jordan. Do you want to be with her?" *Or me.* He didn't have to say the last part. I saw it in his eyes. I hadn't been fast enough with an answer, so he stormed back to the truck, climbed in, and left.

Feeling dumped, again, with my brain still trying to catch up, I dragged my feet to Hector as the parking lot emptied.

"What you feel for my sister."

I didn't feel anything for Jaylene but the need to help her. To find the truth and maybe bring her back to baseline. That's what she'd always said. That I was her baseline. Maybe losing me had set her off. Maybe it'd been my fault that she took it out on Penny. Maybe…I didn't know any more maybes. Just that I needed to find the truth and Penny didn't fit. She hadn't been one of us. Maybe the killer made a mistake. And mistakes led people to do stupid things and get caught. I didn't think Jaylene would kill someone, but she was somehow mixed up in this mess.

Only one car remained in the lot. As if he had been waiting for everyone to leave before pushing out the door, Riley sprinted to his car. I thought he saw me, but then he drove away. I realized then that I needed Riley and Aimee to help me figure things out.

I needed my friends.

I followed Riley home and knocked. Mrs. Eaton opened the door. She was a tall, thin, dark haired woman with kind eyes and a smile she usually gave me whenever she saw me. Except now, she was just tall and thin, and her eyes hardened, and her smile was nonexistent.

"Hi, Mrs. Eaton. I was wondering if I could speak with Riley."

Riley stood behind her, about to climb the stairs to his room. He gave me a wide-eyed look and shook his head slowly. A warning of sorts. I, of course, ignored it. One thing I realized about being odd was that people tended to be polite when you acted dumb. So I acted as if I hadn't caught on to Riley's panic and Mrs. Eaton's blatant disapproval of me and walked past her to Riley with a smile.

"Hey, Riley, do you think you can help me with this math problem like last time? Mrs. B is kicking my butt."

Riley lifted his eyes to his mother. I hoped he wouldn't push me away like last time. He looked more terrified than anything else.

"Ten minutes," Mrs. Eaton said and closed the

door. "And you better hope your father doesn't come home first."

Riley sighed and sprinted up the stairs. I followed him into his room. It was trashed, like always. "Are you crazy?" He spun to me and shook his head. "Don't answer that. You shouldn't be here."

"Are we still friends?"

He made a noise and plopped down on his bed, hugging the pillow in front of him and scooting back to the wall. "I'm not supposed to be friends with you anymore. My dad beat me that night Penny went missing. I didn't do it. We left Quinn's together, but she had me drop her off at Max's. Said she didn't want to go home and was meeting up with some friends. I had a curfew. She didn't. I don't know what happened after that. The cops still think I had something to do with her death. I have to lay low. Stay away from you."

Ouch. That hurt. "I didn't do anything."

"Yeah, but Sheriff Johnson keeps bringing up your name."

"Do you think I did anything to Penny?"

He let out a breath. "No. Of course not. And we thought you were dead too." He cleared his throat and turned to look at something other than me. His eyes gleamed and he wiped them. "We thought you were dead."

I sat down near his legs. "I think Jaylene is involved somehow and I want to break into her house."

Riley didn't say anything at first then he started to laugh. An all-out, not laughing at me, laugh. As if the anger in him had finally burst into a bubble of laughter, he laughed, clenching the pillow in his hands. Tears streamed down his face. I thought it best to put space between us, so I got up and sat at his desk instead until he finished. "Omigod, Jordan, I missed you."

That made me smirk. "I missed you too."

He stopped laughing and kept his eyes on me. "I'm sorry about what I said. I knew if I wasn't mean to you, you wouldn't let things go."

"Well, it still didn't work. We're friends."

He nodded. "Yeah, friends."

"Have you heard from Aimee?"

Guilt touched his eyes, and he lowered them. "No. I messed up big time." He ran his hand through his hair, collecting himself, then sighed before he lifted his eyes to me with a fierce determination that indicated I had my friend back. "What do you need from me?"

"I want you to help me find out what happened to Penny."

Chapter Thirty

We dropped my car off at my house and took Riley's car to the Coopers' house. Jaylene and I had often snuck out at night despite the alarm and cameras in the place. She and I had liked the thrill of being bad and since her parents were so strict with her comings and goings, they had made sure to secure the place. The window above the sloped roof had been disarmed. The edge of the roof was close to the deck's banister. Mr. Cooper's car was the only one in the driveway and his office faced the east side of the house. Away from where I was now lifting my body and dragging myself up the roof, praying I wouldn't fall.

Riley would wait at the library a few miles away for my pickup call. He'd told his mom he had to go check out a book at the library and she had called Mrs. Tanner, the librarian, to ensure his arrival. Although Mrs. Eaton used Mr. Eaton to scare Riley, she was much scarier.

I used a butter knife to wedge the window open and climbed inside. The window led into the second-floor foyer. Thankfully, the plush rug masked the thump of my fall. Once inside, I tiptoed to the hallway leading to Chase's and Jaylene's room. I wondered why their parents had put them across from each other. The place had another bedroom on the other side. To keep Chase safe from Jaylene's tantrums, they could've put him in that bedroom instead. It didn't make sense, and I had never thought about it before. I just liked that Chase was close to her bedroom so I could sneak glances at him whenever I was with Jaylene. Sometimes even enjoy his music. They had also forced him to skip a grade so he'd be in the same graduation class as Jaylene. He'd done it without argument for her. But thinking about it now, it all seemed so unfair for him.

I stopped outside Jaylene's door and stared at it. This mission was doomed if I couldn't even get inside her room. I had hoped it'd be open like last time. Not the case. I had hoped knowing the reason behind my fear of doors would've cured me.

It hadn't.

My heart quickened its pace, my hands started getting sweaty, and my head felt fuzzy. The memories, or more like the impression of what I remembered, slammed into me. I couldn't remember the faces of the people I'd lured behind that door. I could only hear the screams. The terror. The door knocking against the frame as whoever was on the other side tried to break free.

It hadn't ever worked though.

The door started to swell. Blood pooled underneath. It's what my four-year-old self would've imagined behind the door.

A monster.

No. No. Not real. This wasn't real.

But it felt real to me. I shut my eyes and pulled out of my mind, concentrating on the other noises around me. The front door opened and closed. Loud booted beats followed and then voices.

"What are you doing here?" Mr. Cooper asked.

"You haven't been answering. We have a big fucking problem." That voice belonged to Sheriff Johnson.

Then they moved to the study. Or somewhere else. I breathed slowly, every inch of my body breaking out in goosebumps. I heard muffled voices, movement, and then I opened my eyes to Penny standing in front of me. Her skull caved. Blood caked her face. Her eyes lost all color and were glazed in filmy white. Dead. She lifted her hand as if to poke me and I violently flinched and stumbled back into Chase's door. If flung open. I may have squealed as I lost my balance and fell on my ass making enough noise to paint a target on my head.

The time it took for me to land on my ass and look up, Penny was gone.

But footsteps started up the stairs. Heavy and fast. I skittered back and kicked the door closed. I jumped to my feet and ran to the bathroom, closing that too. A mistake. A damn mistake. I locked myself inside and climbed into the tub, my back to the wall, staring at the door.

The closed door.

I heard the bedroom door slam open, and then the bathroom doorknob jiggle. Then an open palm slam. "Who the fuck is there?" Sheriff Johnson said. "Open the fucking door or I will break it."

"Jack, what is wrong with you?" Mr. Cooper said in a calm voice.

Then a third voice popped up. "What the hell are you doing in my room?"

Chase.

"Son," Mr. Cooper said, using that same calm voice. "Who's in your room?"

Shit. No. No. I had to do something, but I couldn't open the door. I couldn't. I couldn't.

"Jordan," he finally said. "I told him to meet me here."

"In a minute," I said. "I'm using the bathroom."

A few minutes later, footsteps retreated out of the room and then a soft knock on the door followed. The knob wiggled. "Jordan, you have to unlock the door so I can open it."

I knew that. But I still couldn't move. "I can't," I said, my voice shaking. "She's out there."

I heard him sigh and something tap on the door. His forehead. "Jay's not here."

I shook my head. "Not Jaylene. Penny."

Silence stretched for a long time, and then the knob started to shake again. This time it popped out and fell on the floor. Chase swung the door open. *Chase* not Penny. He took one look at me and whatever anger he had vanished. He didn't move inside. He didn't yell. He didn't tell me I was crazy. He looked right in my eyes and saw something that made him care.

"Penny isn't here either." He leaned on the door, not crowding me, letting me figure things out. With the door wide open, I could see his bedroom. "It's just you and me."

I finally unclenched my hands and ran them over my thighs. The rough feel of denim against my palms cleared away the haze. Deep breaths helped too.

He took a step back into the room. The door yawned open. I managed to find enough feelings in my legs to climb out of the tub. I probably should've stayed in the bathroom because now he did look angry.

"I would ask what you are doing here, but I don't think I want to know. Let's get out of here before I change my mind and give you up to Sheriff Johnson for trespassing."

I followed in his wake, keeping up with his long strides. Mr. Cooper wasn't around, and neither was Sheriff Johnson. "Does the sheriff visit your dad a lot?" I asked, glancing around the room to make sure Jack Johnson wasn't listening in. I didn't realize Chase had stopped moving until I slammed into him.

He kept his hands at his sides. "Johnson doesn't approve of Finn dating Jaylene. Says she's distracting him from football." Chase narrowed his eyes on me. "Anything else you'd like to know?"

Yeah. Johnson might have tried to kill me the other night. I couldn't manage that though, so I sheepishly shook my head.

Without another word, we walked outside. Chase climbed into his truck, and I didn't move, unsure if I should walk home or hop in. Leaning to the passenger door, he pushed it open. I got in. I texted Riley to let him know I'd been busted, and Chase was taking me home. Or somewhere to slaughter me. I wasn't sure yet.

I recognized the road. Home. He stopped in front of my house, but I didn't get out right away. It was peaceful here. Lonely.

"I don't get you," he said to the windshield because he didn't want to look at me. "You reject your perfect half, but you're always staring at her as if she actually hurt you. Then you kiss me and we..." he wiped his face. "We made love, and you still have this infatuation with her. You just can't let her go."

He used love, not sex. We had made love. It made my heart swell but the words I wanted to say got stuck in my throat.

"And I still can't get you out of my head. I liked you since the night of the storm. The night we got stuck in the basement in my house and the lights went out. I was so scared, trying to act all cool about it, but you kept your head straight. We found candles and matches. You told me what to do. To breathe. And all I kept thinking was how brave you were even though you were terrified of the door." He chuckled.

I remembered that night. I was in sixth grade. Five years ago! He liked me five years ago. "I thought you hated me."

"I wasn't supposed to feel this for you. For one: you're a guy. The thought of me being queer kinda freaked me out. And for two: my parents made it very clear that I had to stay away from you. Even as friends. You belonged to Jay. Like her plaything. She'd formed an attachment to you when she hadn't ever had an attachment with anyone. She was happy around you. So different than with me and my parents. It killed me every time. So," he shrugged. "I started just acting like an ass. I wanted to be the opposite of her so my parents could see me too." He raked his hand down his face.

I wanted to say the perfect words to let him know that I didn't like Jaylene. That I liked him. A lot. "I should go," I said instead.

He nodded, still not looking at me. I opened the door to climb out when I heard him say, "I thought being with Tabatha would stop me from feeling things for you. It didn't."

I couldn't move and turned back to him. This time he speared me with his blue, sad eyes. "Would you like some chocolate?" I blurted like an idiot. Then I shook my head, hopped down the truck, and slipped inside my empty house before he could respond. Or laugh at me.

Stupid. Stupid. Stupid.

Chocolate. Really? I leaned against the closed door and wanted the pounding inside my head to stop. It didn't. Then someone knocked on my door and I opened it. Chase stood there in all his brilliance.

"I don't like Jaylene like that. I never had. I just worry about her. I promise. I like you," I blurted out the word vomit and kept going. "A lot," I added, in case it wasn't clear. He took a step inside, and I had to take a step back. He closed the door behind him. "I like listening to your music." He stepped closer, I stepped back. "I like the way you wear your hair."

"My hair?" he said with a smirk, still walking closer.

"Yeah. It's nice. And your eyes. You have

beautiful eyes."

"I do?"

I nodded. "Yeah." I stopped moving when my back hit the kitchen counter. He stopped just inches from me.

"I like you too, Jordan. A lot."

He leaned in and stopped just a hair's breadth away from my lips. He waited for me to decide. It only took a heartbeat. I pressed my lips to his and everything else slipped away.

ELIZABETH ARROYO

Chapter Thirty-One

Unsure of the secret code Chase passed to me via looks at school, I gave up trying to snatch time with him and drove to Liam's house afterward as instructed. Basil met me at the door with Mrs. Grant. After a short greeting, I followed Basil to Liam's room where he sat at his desk killing his keyboard. He gave me his angry look making me feel all sorts of guilty.

"Where have you been?" he asked sharply.

"Around."

Liam snorted. "He's distracting you."

The accusation made my defenses rise. "He's not."

"Did you even think about what we should do about, you know, being on some serial killer's list?"

Nope.

"Exactly. He's distracting you."

Considering no one else knew about me and Chase, I was starting to think Liam was some sort of mind reader. Chase and I had decided to keep our thing a secret. He wasn't ready to come out and quite honestly, neither was I. I wasn't sure about anything right now, except that I liked him a lot. Liam was right. I didn't want to think of anything else. Like being on some kind of serial killer list. Like being dead. Like my dad being some FBI agent.

"Did you decide what you're going to do?" he asked, finally releasing the keyboard from the torture and planting his hands on his lap.

I plopped on the bed. "No." Ever since Liam found out I was Basil, he'd been different. As if searching for something he'd lost. He sidled into bed beside me.

"Are you okay?" I asked him.

"Not really. I mean, it's been ten years and therapy helped make sense of things, but for someone to blame us for what we did when the outcome wouldn't have mattered anyway, to kill us off as if we weren't..." His voice trailed off.

As if we weren't victims too.

The memories of my time with the Batemans were still fuzzy and wobbly. Where Liam had ten years to figure it all out in his head, I'd had days. I didn't know which was better. Most of the information I had, I'd gleaned from Dakota's book. According to Dakota, the Parents always killed their mark with or without our help. Matthew hadn't been the only kid who had tried to save us. "But we know we're being hunted," I said, trying for a positive spin. "This gives us an advantage, right?"

"Yeah, I guess."

A sudden compulsion had me climbing into bed with him and curling on my side. He'd given me his arm so I could rest my head. I remembered this. Out of everything, I remembered Kale. I curled up close to him and he wrapped a secure arm around me. "We're family, right?"

I couldn't see his face, but I could tell he was fighting the urge to cry. "Yeah," he answered softly.

"And we protect each other. We'll always come back."

I felt his forehead against my temple. "We're the only ones left, Basil."

The name made me stiffen and we fell asleep that way, like we used to when we were kids in a cage with serial killers.

I woke up first and peeled out of his arms. I watched him sleep for a long time, remembering. He was two years older and bigger than me, and he'd always let me sleep on him. He had protected me. Now it was my turn.

I drove Hector into the cold November afternoon. The sky was already a touch pink on the horizon. I reran everything I knew about what my gut was telling me, and it led me back to Jaylene. There was something at the edge of my mind I had to grasp but couldn't. Something I was missing. Like a word at the edge of your tongue you couldn't quite remember.

It all floated into the air when I got home, and Vicky's car was missing. The overwhelming feeling of being abandoned settled over my heart. She could've returned me, but she hadn't. Not yet. I had no family. No one.

But you do have family, Jordan. Just look inside Teddy. The answer is right there.

I wanted to invite Chase over and forget everything. Just be with him.

Headlights cut a path through the windows and I wondered if Chase was a mind reader too. I opened the door like a fool, but it wasn't Chase. Sheriff Johnson hopped down from his truck, wearing an expression that meant business. I thought he was going to plow me over when he kept walking, forcing me to let him inside the house.

"What are you doing here?" I snapped.

"Where's Vicky?" he snapped.

I clenched my hands at my sides just to keep from pointing a finger at him. He had hurt her. But I wasn't going to tell him that. "At work."

He continued into her bedroom. I followed him, looking over his shoulder, wishing she were asleep on the bed. She wasn't. "She hasn't returned my calls."

"Maybe she needs time away from *you*." The finger almost made an appearance.

He glared at me. His anger surfacing, his face morphing into something very, very dangerous. "Stop being a little shit. I know this change in her has something to do with you."

"Me? I didn't do anything. You're the one who broke her heart." I regretted saying that the moment his expression took a downward turn, as if he regretted it too. Then he remembered me and glared at me as if trying to figure something out. Deciding I wasn't worth the effort, he headed for the door. But then he stopped, his hand on the edge of the door, shoulders tensed. I sucked in a breath suddenly wondering if I'd allowed a killer into my house. And I was alone. He'd been angry at Mr. Cooper about something. Could it be Jaylene? Did Sheriff Johnson know about Jaylene but said nothing?

He turned to look at me over his shoulder. "Tell her to call me."

I nodded. I'd agree to anything just to get him out of my house.

He walked out and I quickly secured the door, my heart pounding hard against my chest. *Relax, Jordan. Not everyone is a serial killer.* No, but I'd always be in danger and so would Liam. Ignoring it didn't make it go away. We were on borrowed time, and I had to do something. I found Teddy where I left him on the desk and dropped on my bed. I pulled out Special Agent Nate Martinez's business card and compared it to the number I pulled out from the secret zippered compartment under Teddy. The card was old, weathered, but the writing was clear. The numbers were different. I felt a sting of disappointment that Liam had been wrong. Special Agent Nate Martinez wasn't my dad. There was something about the agent that made me want him to like me. Something familiar.

I played with Teddy's card in my hand.

Man up.

Learn the truth.

Survive and make sure Liam survived.

I dialed the number.

It rang and rang. I almost hung up when a man's voice answered. A voice through space and time, discombobulated from a body. I tried to imagine the features attached to the rumbly voice belonging to a man that might or might not be my dad. My memories of my childhood were a whirlwind of imaginary images mixed with truth. I couldn't pull them apart.

"Hello?" the grumbly man said. "Who is this?"

Everything I meant to say disappeared. Hanging up suddenly felt like the right choice. So why couldn't I do it? Just hang up. Disconnect the call. Do not answer.

"I know you're there. I can hear you breathing. Who the fuck is this?"

Wow, Dad had no patience. I almost giggled. "You first. Who are you?"

"Hey, buddy," he snapped. "You're the one who called me. How the hell did you find this number?"

"In a hidden compartment inside my teddy bear." There was no answer for a long time, and I thought he hung up on me. I had to look at my phone to be sure.

"Jordan? Is this you?"

The voice on the other end of the call suddenly sounded familiar. The image of Special Agent Nate Martinez swam in front of me. *"Bellamy would've been your age,"* he'd said. His son. The one who died when he was six years old.

Six.

The same age I'd been when my mom abandoned me.

I remembered the way he looked at all those pictures of the missing kids on the sheriff's wall. As if he were looking for one in particular.

Bellamy. Me. I was Bellamy.

For a moment, my brain tried to capture when he'd figured it out and I remembered the hospital. They'd drawn blood, taken evidence. DNA. That had been weeks ago. I closed my eyes and drew up all the memories I could of my mom. Of my real Mom. "I remember Mom smelled like flowers and her smiles were always sad. I remember cake for breakfast because if you eat it first, it is breakfast. Was that real?" I couldn't stop talking now that I was on a roll. "I remember Nana. She saved my life. Was she real?"

"Yes," he answered. "That was real."

"What happened to Nana?"

"She passed away a few years ago."

Something dark pushed through the pulsing beat in my chest and knotted all my insides. He'd kept the dog but discarded me. He'd left town knowing I was his son. The argument he had with Vicky the day he left made sense. He'd been angry that he found me. He'd taken it out on the steering wheel inside his car.

And that hurt. A lot.

"You knew," I heard myself saying from a distance. "You knew I was your son, and you still left."

I heard the muffled sound of movement on his end of the phone. "Daddy!" A little girl in the background screeched. "We're going to be late, and you promised."

"Babe, we're going to be late." The sound of a woman's voice followed.

I remembered how he talked to me at Wally's Mart condom aisle. How he had handed me that disgusting bar and the way he kept telling me to be safe. I'd wanted him to like me for reasons I couldn't explain. To like *me*. But he thought I could be Penny's killer.

He'd lied about keeping me safe after I'd been found. He'd left me and Mom and made a brand-new family because I was broken.

"You *lied*," I spat, remembering other things he had said after they'd found me and brought me home. "You said I'd be safe. You said you'd protect me. You said you'd never let me go, but you did. You lied! You went ahead and made a new family. You buried me and I wasn't even dead!"

"No, Bellamy, that's not true."

"I'm not Bellamy!" I couldn't hold back the tears now. But they were tears of pain, of anger, of something I had buried deep inside and had never been able to let out. "They're killing us," I said dryly. "Peppermint, Caper, Rosemary, they're all dead. And you left me." He started to say something, but I hung up.

I heard Vicky come in that night. I wanted to talk to her about everything, but she didn't check up on me. And the next morning, she was gone.

ELIZABETH ARROYO

Chapter Thirty-Two

Hector smelled like pine trees and disinfectant. He started up easily despite the cold temperatures. At least I had him. Reliable now so that I may creepily follow Chase, an easy target. His truck was larger than life. He hadn't answered my texts or calls, so I'd been forced to follow him through the winding streets. SA Nate Martinez hadn't called me back since our talk yesterday, but I knew he was coming for me and then everyone would know I was Bellamy Martinez, groomed to be a serial killer. I had to come clean with Chase before he heard it from someone else. I had to break open all my truths and hope that he'd still love me.

Love me?

My heart hurt just thinking about love. Did he love me at all? Could he love someone like me?

My thoughts were cut short when he made a sharp right into an unpaved path, and I followed quickly slamming the brakes just in time to avoid crashing into his tailgate.

Busted.

He jumped out of the truck and approached my window. I couldn't be sure if he was amused or angry. "What are you doing?"

I lowered my window. "Following you," I answered. "You haven't answered my calls."

He lifted one finger. "You called and texted once. Only once."

I shrugged. "And you didn't answer."

He did that Jack Johnson thing where he looked up into the sky as if searching for answers before dragging his glare back to me. "Follow me."

"Duh."

He chuckled on his way back to his truck. I liked that sound a little bit too much. It kinda cracked my heart a little bit. The narrow road led to a small cabin at the edge of a lake. Chase quickly parked the truck on the side and rushed inside as if needing to hide the bodies. I slowly got out of Hector and looked beyond the lake at the mountains looming against the skyline. The sight was beautiful and frightening. I imagined being lost in those mountains. Alone. And realized it was exactly how I felt now. Lost and alone. I needed to get all the stuff in my head out. I needed Chase.

When Chase came back outside, I felt stiff and cold. I was also rubbing the spot above my heart. "Are you coming inside?"

"Do you want me to come inside?"

He cocked his head and grabbed my cold hand. Then he led me inside. I gave the place a slow perusal. It was small and clean with just a worn tan sofa, a square wood table with four chairs, and a kitchen. A narrow hallway must've led to the bathroom and bedroom in the back. And all the doors were open.

I smiled at him. Couldn't help it. He'd opened the doors for me. I dropped my backpack on the sofa and followed his lead, taking off my shoes and coat. The fire already warmed up the place. "Where are we?" I asked.

"Cabin," he answered. The *duh* implied.

"Why are you here?" I stood behind the counter and watched as he started taking out sandwich condiments from the fridge and cupboards. He worked meticulously. Not random at all. I loved watching him move. It made sense. He made sense to me.

"It was my mom's place."

"Was?"

He didn't answer. Just made the sandwich and

handed me one. When he was done, he cleaned everything, returned it, and led me to the sofa. "I come up here when I need quiet time to write."

He disappeared into one of the rooms and came back out with a guitar. Smirking at me, he sat on the plush rug on the floor, the guitar across his lap, leaning against the sofa near my feet. Then he started to play.

I pulled out my sketchbook and pencils from my backpack with an itch to draw him and sat on the floor opposite him. I took in everything about him. His hair pulled into a messy bun, the curve of his jaw, his nose, chin. His eyes, half lidded in concentration to the music floating from his instrument. I absorbed it all in and it took a moment to solidify the image in my head and then I started to draw.

I'd only ever drawn him when I was alone in my room. I'd never drawn in front of anyone. So lost in his features, I missed when he stopped playing and sidled next to me, watching me work. At least until I finished shading in the liner around his eyes and I looked up from the sketchbook to him staring at me. I couldn't move or look away. The awed look in his expression forever seared into my brain. A slow smirk lifted the corner of his mouth, and he leaned into me for a kiss. A gentle touch that meant more to me than the whole world.

"Has anyone ever told you, you look handsome when you're lost in your head?"

"No," I said.

He kissed me again. A fast peck I chased as he pulled away. He chuckled. "Well, you do." He sat back next to me and took my hand in his. The touch felt so right. "So, why were you stalking me?"

I didn't want to ruin this with my truths, but I had no choice. I had no time. I wasn't sure what Special Agent Martinez would do to me once he came to get me.

If he came at all. Who would ever want a broken boy?

"Hey." Chase cupped my chin, so I had to look at him. Concern laced his words. "Tell me."

I put my notebook down and pulled out Caper's book from my bag. Chase's whole demeanor changed as he watched. His face paled, the smile gone, and his eyes cold. I offered him the book, but he quickly got to his feet as if it were an infection he didn't want to catch.

"What the fuck is this?" he snapped.

I got to my feet too, with the book still in my hands. I couldn't speak, unsure why he was so mad. "There's something I have to tell you," I managed to get out.

He yanked the book from my hands and tossed it into the fireplace. The pages quickly caught and curled in the flames. "Get out," he ordered, voice cracking.

I didn't move. I couldn't. "I just wanted to know the truth." He had to understand that much.

"Why? What difference does it make? She's dead."

I clamped my mouth shut, suddenly realizing that we weren't talking about the same thing. Chase dropped onto the sofa, leaned forward, and cupped his face in his hands. Then he started to cry. I dropped to my knees in front of him, afraid to touch him, but I touched him anyway. "Chase, please, talk to me."

After a few minutes, he dragged in a deep breath. "She was number six. My mom. The last. Her body was still her when they found her. Her grave was the only one exposed out of the other five."

I heard him through the pounding beat of my heart and the shallow intake of breaths I'd managed to take. I knew number six. She'd been the grave Sage had hidden me in. The body that had covered mine. I'd been buried with her.

"They took her when she was with Jay," he went on without looking at me. "We found Jay roaming the woods after three days. Three days. She'd been four years old. That's why she's the way she is. It's not her fault. Dad tried therapy but it never made her whole again." He ran his hand down his face. "Then the book came out. All of it so damn horrible. It felt like I was reliving it over and over again. Jay got worse. By the time she returned from her summer college tours, she was already decompensating. Then…"

He didn't have to add the then part. Then I rejected her.

"I just…I never understood it. I read that the kids were kept in cages, that they were forced to lure victims, but how could they do it? How could one life be worth more than another? And none of them were charged. They got out free when they should've paid for what they did alongside the Batemans. They should've *paid*." Anger pinched his features and he got to his feet and walked as far away from me as he possibly could. "My dad worked for the victims' families. They wanted to charge the kids as adults. Those kids weren't worth saving." He shook his head. "They weren't," he said softer as if trying to convince himself. "They were damaged anyway. They'd probably go on to commit crimes too. But we got no justice."

Although still in the same room, I felt as if we were now a planet apart. Unreachable. The words I had meant to spill, the truths I had meant to figure out with him, collapsed behind my torn heart. I had no defense other than being afraid for myself and for Liam. Other than knowing that the Batemans would've killed them anyway. That we always held out to hope that one of them would've saved us. I'd been a kid who knew nothing else. Was I still that kid? Would I do it all over again to protect those I loved? Was I evil because of it? There were a slew of families who hated us. Were they right? Were we monsters? I thought about how I'd wanted to hurt Steel, how I saw myself hurt Tabatha, about the dark stain I felt in my soul. No. No. I didn't want to believe that. I couldn't. Liam wasn't a monster. I wasn't a monster.

"They were just kids," I blurted. *I was just a kid.*

"So was I! You have no idea what it's like to live in that house with a sick sister who I'm afraid of! Sometimes I think she's planning *my* murder. Do you have any idea what that's like? And my stepmom, she tells me to be patient. Dad tells me to suck it up. They let her do whatever she wants to *me*. And I let her, so she doesn't hurt herself. So what more truths do you want, Jordan?" he asked, wiping the tears from his face. "Is that good enough for you?"

The silence between us stretched into something like the end. I didn't know how to fill it or what to say to make it better. I narrowed the wide gap between us. He straightened, stiffened in his posture, but I didn't stop until I drew him into my arms and hugged him tighter than I have ever hugged him. It took a few seconds for him to finally relax and hug me back. "I'm sorry," I said. The words weren't enough to heal us. They weren't enough to change us. But they were the only ones I could offer.

Chapter Thirty-Three

Liam paced. At this rate, he'd wear out his socks in a few hours. Mrs. Grant had us both leave our shoes in the mud room. The beats of his footsteps were oddly soothing. After I left Chase at his mom's cabin—he wanted to be alone—I didn't have anywhere else to go. Riley was still on a Jordan lockdown and Aimee wasn't answering her calls. Liam, however, had his anxiety spiked to an all-time high.

"Six families could be on that suspect list," Liam finally said.

I told him what Chase said about the families wanting justice. Any number of those could've been the killer.

"Including Chase," he added.

As if I hadn't been thinking about that all this time. "He doesn't know who I am."

Liam stopped pacing. A sort of calmness came over his features. "You're right. They don't know who we are. You're not even Bellamy anymore. And I was adopted. My papers sealed. My adopted parents changed my name. There's no way they can find out who we are." His celebratory smile fell when he looked at me. "What? What did you do?"

"I called Special Agent Nate Martinez and uh, he knows about me. I kinda hung up on him. And, um, I think Vicky knows."

Liam stopped mid-pace and stared at me. It wasn't until Basil whinnied and brushed against his leg that Liam blinked out of whatever haze he'd been under and started moving again. I didn't even think he realized he'd turned to stone for a few seconds. He fell on the bed.

"Shit."

"That's why I wanted to tell Chase about me. If Special Agent—"

"Shit, Jordan. Just call him Nate. He's your dad."

"—Special Agent Martinez reveals who I am. I'm dead."

Liam gave me his most pathetic look. He really had beautiful eyes. "Or bait."

On second thought. He was nuts. I got to my feet and started to pace. "Are you serious right now?"

He got to his feet and stopped me from pacing which I thought was unfair considering I let him pace. "Bait is better than being clueless. We can do something to protect the bait."

I shrugged out of his hold. "Like what?"

"We can arm you."

I snorted. "With a gun?"

"Mace, a small blade in your boot." He pointed at my socks. "Something." The pacing continued. "What about a tracking chip? Basil has one."

"Ugh." I dropped back on the bed and felt it shift as Liam climbed on with me. The sudden compulsion to burrow myself against him just to feel safe almost had me rolling over. Feelings I didn't think I had for him settled over me. I felt his fingers brush my hair like he used to do. "We're going to be okay," he said.

The same thing I told him for so many nights as we shared a prison. I hadn't known what it meant to be okay, but I felt okay with him. I had to stop feeling. Between Chase hating me and Liam wanting to use me as bait, *feelings* were going to get me killed. "Well, if I'm bait we better hurry up and think of something because if Special Agent Martinez pulls me out of the state, I'm screwed."

"You think he'll just take you?"

I shrugged. "He hates me. He probably wants to lock me up."

Liam didn't say anything to that, and I didn't know what to think.

"I have an idea. But we're going to need help. Do you have anyone you trust? Like really trust." I opened my mouth to say Chase, but he beat me to it and said, "Not Chase."

I sat up. "He's not a killer."

"No, maybe not, but his parents might be. And how long do you think he'd be able to keep that secret?"

Good point. "There's Riley and Aimee."

"Are you sure they're not in this victims' club?"

"Riley's parents are still alive. I'd say no. Aimee lives with her dad who's a deputy chief in the sheriff's office. I don't know what happened to her mother."

Liam arched a brow. "Bad cop?"

"We'll have to ask Riley. He was dating her. He should know."

"Well then, let's go have a convo with your BFF."

Having a convo with Riley sounded easy enough, except that he wouldn't answer his phone, and we staked out his place for two hours before we got hungry and headed for food. We decided on takeout and Liam drove us to the school lot to eat because he didn't want to be anywhere the killers could see him. *Duh.*

"Do your friends usually ditch you?" Liam asked, biting into his burger.

"Yeah, sometimes, so?"

He shrugged. "Shouldn't friends be, like, dependable?"

"Shouldn't you know, having friends and all?" I deadpanned, kinda upset.

He shoved a fry in his mouth making him look like a chipmunk with too many nuts in his cheeks. "I don't really have friends."

"What about Chase and your bandmates?"

"I hang out with them, but we don't talk. Like talk. I think they're afraid of catching my cooties and I'd either turn them gay or have a crush on them."

"That's stupid. They don't care about Chase." I bit my tongue at the slip.

"So, you and Chase, huh." It took him three seconds. I counted.

"You act surprised when you're the one who told me to make a move."

"No, I didn't."

"Uh, yes you did. The night of Quinn's party. You said I better make a move because he never will."

"Yeah, because I didn't think he was *gay*."

I opened my mouth and snapped it shut. I didn't even want to think about the conversation and why I had listened to Liam anyway. He'd been drunk. *I* was stupid. No wonder Chase pushed me away.

"So, he's gay?"

I didn't remember Liam being such a talker. "I'm not going to out anyone." But yeah, he had to be gay, or at least bi. We did things. Shit. Now Liam had me wondering if he used me to trap me into some nefarious scheme to murder me. This convo sucked.

"Well, maybe we can ask him, since he's, uh, here."

I turned to where Liam pointed and saw Chase pull up in his truck. "He's supposed to be in his cabin writing music."

Thankfully, Liam had parked away from the main lot, but we ducked down anyway just in case. "What is he doing here?"

Chase parked next to the building and slipped out of sight near the field. Ignoring Liam's scolding, I got out of his car.

"We are going to get caught."

"Just be quiet." I followed where Chase disappeared to and heard raised voices before catching sight of him and Aimee in a heated argument. Chase looked all kinds of murderous. A change from the sobbing mess I had left in the cabin.

"What are you going to do with it?" Aimee asked nervously.

Chase had something in his hand I couldn't see. "What the hell do you expect me to do with it?"

"Get rid of it."

Chase grabbed Aimee by the throat and shoved her hard. She stumbled back, cupping her neck. "Stay the fuck away from her."

Something in Aimee's eyes sent chills through me. She didn't look afraid. She looked giddy. Like when she got an A in her psych class. Then it was gone, replaced by anger. She spun and stomped away.

Liam tugged me under the bleachers as Chase made his way back to his truck. Their conversation rattled in my brain at least until I felt Liam wrap his arms around me, pulling me tight into him. His heart rattled too but it was for a different reason. His whole body stiffened. I remembered when he'd been in his room. The way he'd turned into a stone statue and Basil had whimpered and helped him out of it. I held onto him too, hoping to bring him back. I couldn't lose him to whatever nightmares still clung to him.

"I can't lose you, Liam," I whispered in his ear. "Come back. Please."

I felt his body go lax in my arms. The moment lasted a second before he pulled sharply away and sprinted back to his car. Without waiting for me, he climbed in. I thought he was going to leave me, so I jumped in right after him. I wanted to ask him what that was about, but Chase was already on the move. "Follow Chase," I said.

"What?"

"Just follow him," I growled.

Muttering something about being a bossy shit under his breath, Liam started the car, and we followed Chase.

After a few minutes of silence, I couldn't hold my tongue. "So, what was that back there?"

He kept his eyes on the road in front of him, making sure not to get too close to Chase. "It's a reaction to stress. I tend to lock down. Basil helps me come back."

"I'm Basil," I said, stupidly.

"I know. It was hard. This whole healing thing. I grew dependent on you. On Basil in the cage. It's just stupid."

It wasn't stupid. I took his hand in mine and squeezed. He let out a shuddering breath. Then he scowled. "Why is he going to Quinn's?"

We came upon Quinn's house, but Chase passed it up. A few miles ahead, he pulled over to the side of the road and we did the same further back so he wouldn't notice us. He got out of his truck like a man on a mission and headed into the woods.

"Where is he going?" Liam whispered.

Realization dawned on me. I knew this place. "He's going to Pike's Pass."

"Why?"

"That's where they dumped Penny's body." I got out of the car and Liam followed me.

"Who dumped Penny's body?"

"They. Them. I don't know who. Stay here. If I don't come back in ten, call Special Agent Martinez and let him know what's going on." Before he could say anything to change my mind, I headed into the woods.

The sun was starting to set. The snow didn't make it any easier to navigate through the landscape quietly. And I had a pebble in my shoe irritating the crap out of me. The bare trees would make it impossible to hide if Chase were to turn around and look for me. He didn't. And I realized why. He had his earbuds on. Music calmed Chase. Lucky for me it also impeded his hearing because I wasn't quiet at all.

He stopped just at the border where the little police flags had been toppled. I hadn't returned since I fell, and I could see it clearly now. My blind run had led me into a steep slope now glazed with ice. I remembered trying to find something to hold on to in the dark and got nothing. It opened up to a hole that led to the cave. I'd been lucky to survive the fall intact.

Chase finally pulled off his buds and shoved them into his jacket pocket, then he took out something small enough to fit in his fist. I couldn't move. My eyes glued to his fisted hand until he opened it.

Penny's bracelet.

"What are you doing?"

He spun, almost slipping, eyes wide, lips parted. His breathing picked up, leaving a plume of breath in the air. "Jordan."

"What are you doing, Chase?" I asked again.

He looked at the bracelet as if wondering how it got there. Then realizing I knew who the owner of that trinket was, he turned his glare on me. "She didn't do it. She'd never hurt anyone. Finn gave it to her."

"Then why are you tossing it? That could have evidence."

"She had it on for weeks. Her DNA will be on it. They won't believe she didn't do it. You know they won't." Because she had a mental illness. He didn't have to say it, but it was there on his face. I remembered how he cried back in the cabin. How everything changed when Jaylene had gotten sick. The way she turned on him. People would believe that she could kill someone, and he'd be the one to purge himself if he lied about it in court. And if he couldn't lie, he'd be the one putting the nail on her coffin.

He took a step toward me, and I instinctively took a step back. For a fraction of a second, I was afraid he'd hurt me, and he knew it. His pained expression said it all. "You think I did it? You think I could hurt you?"

I wanted to say no. But the admission wouldn't come out. "Did you know she knew Natalia Montenegro?"

He scowled. His lips pressed into a thin line. "The dead girl." He shook his head. "You just can't let it go, can you?"

"I'm trying to find out what happened."

"Why? Why are you so damn stubborn about this?"

"Because I was one of them!" I tightened my hands into tight fists. "I was one of the Bateman kids," I clarified. "The one buried with your mom so that I could escape and save the others. Me, Chase. *Me*. I was one of the kids you wanted to punish." Tears pricked my eyes. "I was Basil. I am Basil."

It all clicked for him. Me the enemy. One of *them*. Someone unworthy of forgiveness because he thought we were all messed up and would end up in jail anyway. And I couldn't take it back. I could never take it back.

His eyes lifted to something behind me, and I turned to the newcomer holding a gun.

Chapter Thirty-Four

Death was a natural progression of life. I knew that in my bones. I knew that like I knew my own name. *Ha. Ha. Do you even know your name, Jordan?* I couldn't let Sage back into my headspace. He'd turned bitter. He'd changed from protecting me to admonishing me for all the things I should've done to save those he'd charged me to protect. He'd died for nothing.

The person in front of me had not been my first, second, or tenth choice as villain in this scenario. Her eyes didn't hold that madness I'd seen in my own eyes, they were almost kind.

I'd been a horrible judge of character.

"I'll give you a moment to process it all," Aimee said. "I know it must be a lot to take in. In the meantime, drop your cell phones." Neither Chase nor I moved. Apparently, I needed more time to process. "Now," she ordered, pressing the gun into the back of Liam's head. I heard Chase drop his and I dropped mine.

"Aimee, what the fuck are you doing?" Chase asked.

She forced a tied Liam onto his knees. The gun turned to me. "Yeah, you fucked everything up. I need that bracelet. I came here to kill you and take it so I could blame your sister for Penny, you, and Riley, but here we are."

"*You* killed Penny?" Chase asked. I had to wonder how the hell he thought Aimee got the bracelet in the first place. "You told Finn Penny gave you the bracelet at homecoming. Her way of saying sorry for stealing your boyfriend."

Aimee rolled her eyes, and I almost did the same.

Almost. "Jocks," she mumbled. "And I thought you were smarter." She reached out her free hand. "The bracelet."

Chase glowered and tossed it to her. She caught it easily and shoved it into her pocket.

"In my defense, Penny's death was an accident. She fell and—" She made a snapping noise while cocking her head. I got the gist that Penny hit her head in that fall. I wanted to inform Ms. Insanity that the fall had to have been a hard one if it left her skull shattered. I kept that to myself, deciding it best not to piss her off any more than needed. "Anyway, I heard your convo, so this is good. Really good. Like a two for one deal. Now, come on. We're going on a little trip."

I didn't know much about guns, but I was sure the one she had was real. It looked real. And being the daughter of a cop, she looked like she knew how to use it. Chase and I looked at each other. We weren't close enough yet to read facial expressions, not like I was with Riley, but I knew he was thinking about doing something. With Liam tied, he wouldn't be able to balance himself enough to run. Sure, maybe one of us would survive, but who would make that decision? For a moment, I thought Chase would save himself. Yeah, maybe I had little faith in people. But Chase didn't run. Instead, he squeezed my hand, and I didn't realize how much I needed to know that maybe he still cared about me.

She herded all three of us to her car and forced Chase to open her trunk revealing Riley inside. He lay curled on his side, eyes closed. I couldn't even tell if he was breathing.

"Is he dead?" Chase asked.

"Not yet." She pointed the gun at me. "Get in." I stiffened. Fear shooting straight to my gut. She took one look at me and started to laugh. "Oh, that's right. You don't do well in tight spaces. Even pissed yourself that one time, didn't you?" I felt my cheeks flush. "See, you were the one that gave me the idea of blaming Jaylene for Penny. You told me she threatened Penny, that she was off her rocker, remember? It was your brilliant plan."

I felt sick. So sure it had been Jaylene because she'd been decompensating. She'd been acting out. All because of the book. Chase was right about people not believing Jaylene. I had been one of them.

Chase's *I told you so*, look met my *I'm sorry* expression.

"I even went to Quinn's house that night," Aimee continued. "She told me about your fears of tight spaces. Being buried."

"And you told Steel."

She shrugged. "Guilty. I needed you out of the way. Jaylene was too into you. I think she really liked you." Aimee looked at Chase. "Wonder what she'll think when she finds out you're fucking her brother." She turned a gleaming eye at Chase. "You think she'd finally kill you? I think she would. I honestly think I could spin that one. Along with Penny and this piece of shit." She pointed at Riley.

"And why would she kill me and Liam? How are you going to spin that one?"

She smirked. "She won't be the one blamed for your death. Someone else will."

"How many fucking serial killers live in this fucking town?" Liam snapped.

Aimee didn't have a chance to answer. Riley jerked up, a tire iron in his hand, and struck her as he jumped out of the trunk. I'd never seen him move so fast, look so wild. She stumbled back with a grunt, the gun still in her hand. The jack-in-the box play Riley did had us all jumping away from her as if she were on fire instead of swarming her to overpower her. We lost the

259

element of surprise in two seconds flat. The amount of time it took her to realize she still had the gun in her hand. And she used it. A loud crack cut through the air. The bullet aimed at Riley missed. He and Liam went left while Chase and I went right. Liam with his hands still tied in front of him, stumbled after Riley.

Aimee had two seconds to choose who to follow. She snarled and ran after Riley.

"Don't ever cheat on a serial killer," I mumbled to no one. Chase already went for his truck. No luck though. His tires and Liam's tires were flat. Her car didn't have the keys inside. And we didn't find any cell phones. Our cell phones were in the direction Riley, Liam, and Aimee ran off in.

"Fuck!" Chase roared.

A loud gunshot cracked through the air and all I could think about was Liam. My responsibility. My brother. I couldn't let him die. I started to sprint after them, but Chase pulled me back. "I have to save Liam!"

His expression tightened and he glared at me. Then he plucked the tire iron from the ground and gestured to the woods. "Lead the way."

There was something oddly comforting at having Chase at my back with a weapon. It wasn't a gun, but I was sure he'd be able to swing the tire iron if he had to. And I trusted him. Despite my little freak-out earlier, I did trust him. With my life.

A low whistle from behind me had me stopping and turning to Chase. He pointed at droplets of blood on the snow and took the lead in that direction. He moved silently while I felt as if I were a lumberjack with a pebble in his boot stomping in the woods making enough noise to frighten a flock of birds. No, that wasn't me who scared them into flight. That was the serial killer with the gun.

Chase pulled me down behind a tree. Liam and Riley were crouched behind one too about twenty paces to our left. Liam's hands were free. I followed where they were looking and saw Aimee. She had the gun out in front of her. Batshit crazy. How had I missed it? She was two seconds away from finding them and I knew she wasn't going to take them alive.

I turned to Chase, fisted his collar, and slammed my mouth against his in a clumsy kiss. He didn't open right away, but then he did. I wanted to remember this moment. With him. I wanted to take it with me. I shoved him away, his face a mask of confusion. "I love you," I said. "I know what it feels like now. Thank you." I didn't give him time to react when I jumped to my feet and ran making sure I made enough noise that she'd follow me. A gunshot nearby confirmed that my idiotic plan worked.

I counted how many shots she'd fired. One when Riley hit her. One in the woods, two now. She'd run out of bullets. She had to. Another one rang out and I fell on my hands and knees, my shoulder on fire. I'd been shot! Blood splattered on the white powder. My blood. Adrenaline must've kicked in because I ignored the fire burning my flesh, jumped to my feet, and kept running, hearing her behind me. I didn't intend on going far. And I prayed to Vicky's god that he'd given me more luck than he had empathy.

My blood led her right to me where I stood to make my stand. I didn't feel brave. My body trembled from raw fear. Dying sucked. There was nothing normal about it. And I couldn't stop my brain from reminding me of all those people I helped meet this fate. The ones I had led to the Parents. The ones who had trusted me. I couldn't remember their faces and I didn't know their names, but I could now fill in the blanks of what I'd done. Tears made my vision shimmer and they fell down my face. My fault. I blamed myself for Penny too.

Penny, who had been rolled in a rug and thrown into a hole by Aimee. Aimee? No way Aimee could've done it alone. She had help. Someone strong who carried the body into the woods for her. Someone who could've been a serial killer too.

Aimee didn't have that crazed look of glee in her expression when she approached me. She looked pissed.

"Who!" I yelled at her. "Who helped you with Penny?"

"My father!" she yelled back. "And he's going to forgive me for fucking up when I tell him I put a bullet in *your* head!"

She lifted the gun.

"Aimee, don't!" Chase's voice broke through the sound of my own heartbeat. "I lost my mother too. It doesn't give you the right to do this! He was a victim just like us, just like them!"

Aimee's mother had been a victim and Chase had known. Of course he would've known. His father had led the group that hated us.

I watched Chase for any signs that he was bullshitting. That this was some sort of ploy to save me instead of believing what he was saying, but I only saw compassion and love. I hoped it was love. I really, really did.

"And what about Penny and Riley?" Liam said from her other side. "They weren't part of it."

Aimee snarled but she kept the gun on me. "She was a slut who stole my boyfriend! And where is that cheating bastard, Riley? He deserves to die too!" She turned her cold, insane eyes back to me.

This was it. Aimee was going to kill me.

Then something dark flew past me and slammed into her. She stumbled back and the gun went off. The tire iron bounced off her shoulder and struck a nearby tree. She tried to remain upright but slipped on the ice. I knew where she was headed. I purposely led her here. She started to slip down the slope when I lunged for her, but Chase grabbed my legs, stopping me from following her down. She screamed, her face a mask of fear and terror as she disappeared into the hole. Then everything went silent.

Riley came out of hiding looking like a ghost. His bloodshot eyes wide, his face pale, shivering uncontrollably. "Did I kill her?"

He'd saved my life. Chase gave me a look. I was starting to get better at reading his nonverbal communication. "I'm not sure. We need to find help."

Liam found our phones and made the phone call to emergency services. We were all huddled in Chase's truck waiting for them when it started to snow.

Chapter Thirty-Five

Special Agent Nate Martinez stood leaning in a corner, arms folded over his broad chest, glaring at me as the doctor sewed the back of my shoulder. "You got lucky, young man," Dr. Adman said. I felt him tugging my flesh with the thread. "No bullet. Just debris." I didn't feel particularly lucky.

"Where are my friends?" I hadn't gotten any information from anyone after they split us up in the emergency room. Riley had passed out due to blood loss and had to be taken into intensive care. Aimee had stabbed him in the thigh before she'd drugged him. Fueled with adrenaline, Riley hadn't felt it until we reached Chase's truck to wait for the emergency crew. Liam and Chase were carted away by cops to wait for their parents, and I'd been stuck in a treatment room.

"They're somewhere here, I'm sure. It's been quite a busy night."

If by busy he meant a serial killer teenager trying to kill us, then yeah. I didn't know if Aimee was alive or dead. They had cleared us out of there too fast and nobody wanted to look.

Dr. Adman finished and pulled back. "Keep the sutures clean and dry and see your doctor in a couple of weeks to get them out. You should be fine."

Special Agent Martinez shifted his stance, catching our attention.

"Why is *he* here?" I blurted.

Dr. Adman looked at Special Agent Nate Martinez who wore a deadly expression tempting the older doctor to challenge him. "I'm sorry, sir. Only family is allowed with the patient."

Yay, Dr. Adman. This doctor protection was better than police protection. But then Special Agent Martinez said the words that changed everything.

"I am his father."

I had a Luke Skywalker moment where I wanted to cry out NO! It didn't make it past my mental walls. Dr. Adman turned back to me. "I'm a ward of the state," I said through clenched teeth. "Have you contacted Vicky?" Everyone knew Vicky. This was that type of small town.

"We haven't been able to get through to her. Do you want me to have this gentleman—" He looked nervously at Special Agent Nate Martinez, then back at me. "—escorted out?"

I bet he would've too. Yes was on the tip of my tongue, almost spilled out when Special Agent Martinez lifted his badge. "Mr. Brooks," he said Brooks as if it hurt him to say, "Is under federal custody for murder. Don't impede my investigation, Dr. Adman. You won't like how it ends."

Dr. Adman gulped.

I sighed. "I'm okay, Doc. Special Agent Nate Martinez is with the FBI. I think he's here to gather information or hold up the wall, or something important like that."

Despite the shadows on his face, I could've sworn I caught a hint of a smirk teasing Special Agent Martinez's lips. Then his phone let out a squeal and he picked it up, distracted by the caller.

"I'm okay," I told Dr. Adman again. "Can you just let me know when you get a hold of Vicky?" Her absence started to worry me.

He patted me gently on the shoulder. "The nurse will be in to cover the wound and give you instructions. Then you should be able to go home."

"Thanks."

He walked out and a nurse walked in. Special Agent Martinez kept his glare on her until she finished bandaging my wound as if expecting her to tell him to leave or something as he simultaneously growled at the caller. "Widen the parameter. No, I don't want Johnson leading it. I don't care if it's one of his. This is our jurisdiction, remind him of that." His words could slice paper. There was a slight pause, and he pressed his fingers to his forehead in a barely there show of fatigue. "No, I'm with him now. Just tell her I'll call her when things settle. Thanks."

I felt my cheeks heat up. He was talking about me and probably his wife. His new family. He hung up.

The nurse collected her garbage and walked out.

"You don't have to stay here," I said. I shouldn't have been hurt by the fact that he'd moved on with a new family. I didn't know him. Want to know him. I wanted him to leave.

"I know," he said.

He was irritatingly brief with words. I found mine, surprisingly. "Are you going to explain how I ended up Jordan Brooks in White Falls?" I said the words to the wall at the same time a call came through on his phone. "After you promised to protect me. Your son. Who'd been kidnapped and tortured?" I added that last bit out of spite. It worked for about a second before he fixed his face.

He answered the call.

I jumped off the cot ready to leave. Walk. Move. Bury something. I just needed to get away from him.

"I'll call you back," he said into the phone and then to me, "Jordan, wait."

I stopped just outside the divider realizing I had nowhere to go. If Vicky truly left me, I had no one in the whole world. I turned back inside, this time leaning against the cot, staring at my ugly shoes with the pebble bothering the shit out of me.

"After we found you," he started, his voice edgy. It's the only way I could describe it. Like he was containing his anger or hiding something. "Your mother believed it best to keep you secluded from the media and bad press. Some of the victim families wanted blood. It was a bad time for everyone."

I snorted. "Really? Finding us, Matthew dying, was a bad time?"

He cocked his head, his dark eyes going softer. "That's not what I meant." He ran his hand through his hair. Maybe I was being unfair, but I was tired of being blamed. I blamed myself enough. "Your mother was a forensic psychiatrist. Do you know what that means?"

"Yeah, I'm not stupid," I shot back, though I wasn't really sure except that a psychiatrist meant a head doctor.

"After the trial, she begged me to relinquish my rights as your father. To give her full custody so she could take you away. Change your name, get away from the chaos. She believed that—" He paused and cupped his mouth as if needing time to find the right words. "What you experienced as a kid would lead to trauma."

"Duh."

"Not just trauma."

Then what he was trying to say caught fire in my brain. "She thought I was going to turn psycho."

He didn't move. Stone statue mode perfected but he didn't have to. "You were having episodes. Too young to diagnose as psychopathy. She didn't want to risk it. She thought if you forgot the incident, if she could help you forget, you'd have a better chance at living a normal life."

"Then why didn't you let her take me?"

A hint of pain flashed in his eyes. "Because she wanted me to sever all ties with you. I'm your father."

"But you have another family. You didn't need me." The last part sounded like a squeak. I swallowed the wedge in my throat. "And she did it anyway."

That small emotion he showed for a heartbeat vanished, and the stone-cold version of him returned. "Yes, she did."

I picked at the blood under my nails just to do something. "What, uh, what happened to her?"

"We found her car in a river. Empty. Your car seat was underwater. The straps shredded. Three days later, her body washed up on a bank. Two fishermen reported it in. We looked for your body, but…" he let it hang. Obviously, I hadn't been inside the car. "After we found Penny, I confirmed who you were. I also dug deeper into how she did it. Apparently, she used an alias. She had official birth certificates and social security numbers made for you and her. She staged the accident. Something must've gone wrong. She drowned and you were assumed to have drowned with her. I never looked because I thought you were dead." He turned his face away from me before I could catch any emotion, as if he didn't want me to see him as a real person.

"Why would she bring me here, to White Falls, when this is where everything happened?" My mom had lived in New York. I had lived in New York, taken from a park when I was two years old. I was with the Batemans for two years before Sage's plan freed us. Their base of operations was here, in White Falls. My mother bringing me here when she wanted me to forget what happened made no sense.

"I don't know," he answered.

"Am I so different now than when I was a kid?

You didn't recognize me when we met."

He leaned against the wall and crossed his arms in front of him. "I recognized your eyes. But I thought it was just me. Not the first time I saw your eyes on another kid."

"And you still thought I could kill Penny."

And he didn't offer an apology because despite what he said about my psychopathy or whatever, he believed I could be a killer. At least he didn't lie about it. Instead, when his phone rang again, he answered.

I wanted to cry but at that moment Chase walked into the room. Our eyes met and I found the sun, stars, and moon all in one shot. He didn't hesitate to narrow the gap between us and wrap his arms around me. I didn't hesitate either and felt as if I could finally breathe

Chase kissed the top of my head. "It took me forever to find you. These assholes have us on lockdown."

"I know," I mumbled into his shoulder. "I just want to go home."

He held me tighter, protectively. At least until Special Agent Nate Martinez cleared his throat from his spot under the shadows in a corner. Chase practically burst out of his skin at the surprise, letting me go. After realizing it wasn't some homicidal teenager in the room, he let out a relieved breath while I wanted to cry. Were we hiding? Were we something? Maybe I shouldn't have hugged him. Then he took my hand as if it were the most natural thing in the world and pulled me by his side again. "Uh, who are you?" Chase looked at me for an answer.

"This is Special Agent Nate Martinez of the FBI," I explained.

"I'm his father," Special Agent Martinez said.

There it was again. The father thing.

The space between Chase's brow creased as if expecting some joke. Nope. No joke. "Well," he said. "I'm his boyfriend."

I almost swallowed my tongue. "Boyfriend?"

"Well, you *did* proclaim your love for me."

"That was under duress."

"Yeah." Chase spun me so we were facing each other and cupped my face. "And you will never, ever, fucking ever, do that shit again." Then, despite Special Agent Martinez being in the same room, and stating he was my father, Chase Cooper kissed me.

It was a sweet "we're alive" kiss that brought tears to my eyes. It also made Special Agent Martinez excuse himself to give us some privacy.

"Works every time," Chase said smiling.

Oddly enough, his smile pushed all the dark away and I found myself smiling too. "Is that why you did it? To get me alone?"

"Yeah." Then he leaned in to kiss me for real. A kiss that made my toes curl. That was totally a thing I didn't believe could actually happen.

When the kiss broke, we leaned into each other, our foreheads touching, breathing each other in. Alive. We were alive. "We're going to be okay," he whispered.

I could only nod by that point. I wasn't sure I'd ever be okay. "Are Liam and Riley okay?"

He nodded, but his face tightened a little bit. "Yeah, Riley's staying overnight. They had to flush his system, but he'll be okay. His parents are with him now and Liam went home with his parents. I'm just waiting for Colleen."

His stepmother.

"Aimee?" I asked.

"She's alive. They brought her in. But I don't know. It doesn't look good." He tightened his arms around me. "I'm so sorry, Jordan."

I didn't know exactly what he was sorry for, but it didn't matter because when you loved someone, forgiving their imperfections was easy.

"I'm sorry, too."

He squeezed my hand and the silence between us felt okay. We were going to be okay. I had to believe that.

"Your dad is pretty scary," he said.

I wanted to roll my eyes. I didn't. Dr. Cooper popped her head in. "Let's go, kiddo. We have an early day tomorrow."

"They're going to give us time to rest before they take our statements about what happened."

I wish someone would explain to me what happened. "Okay. Then I'll probably see you there."

He gave me a kiss on the forehead before he walked out.

Boyfriend.

Chase Cooper was my boyfriend. I was too tired to sort through the jumbled emotions spurring to the surface. Special Agent Martinez was nowhere to be found, and I couldn't stay in that room. I walked outside. The cold quickly burrowed into my bones, and I shivered. I should've brought my coat.

It was quiet outside. Too cold for anyone to be out. I took a deep aching breath, closing my eyes to feel. Everything hurt. My soul and my body, but I survived.

That thought darkened as soon as a pinch of pain burned my neck. I opened my eyes to see a man in a dark hoodie. My heart suddenly felt as if it were pounding through tar. My blood was thick and heavy like the rest of me. My legs folded and he grabbed me before I fell.

"I've got you," he said, his voice toxic like the poison he'd injected me with.

I didn't lose consciousness, just the ability to move. I don't know how he managed to get me in his car without anyone stopping him. And I don't know how long we drove for, or in what direction. The Batemans used to put us in the back of a van for hours and drive, then they'd tell us we were in some place exotic like Russia or Canada. I'd been three. Everywhere was exotic. They wanted to confuse us, so we wouldn't run. There was nowhere to run. The world was too big.

I opened my eyes, disoriented until I blinked away the haze. I was lying on an old mattress on the floor. The walls were old brick, chipping and peeling like the dead left out under the sun. Three small cages lined one wall, opposite me. Beyond a brick archway lay two identical doors. Both doors were made of dark heavy wood with a gleaming silver-plated doorknob and no window.

I knew one of the doors led to the stairs and outside. The other door led to the room with the screams.

My heart started to beat too fast, my head began to spin.

Memories filled the space around the darkness of my mind but I couldn't reel them all in. I couldn't remember it all. Only how I felt.

Afraid.

And so damn cold.

I was back at the Batemans' place.

ELIZABETH ARROYO

Chapter Thirty-Six

"They're going to get rid of us," Caper whispered. "They don't let us out anymore. We're no longer useful to them. They're going to put us behind the door and grab younger ones."

I burrowed myself into Kale who always felt warmer than me. Teddy squashed between us.

"Maybe one of them will save us," Kale said. "Maybe someone we bring will save us." He ran his fingers through my hair.

No one said anything to that. So far, no one had saved us. I shut my eyes hard until they hurt. It didn't do nothing for my ears though.

"I won't let them hurt us anymore," Sage whispered.

The ghost sounds of creaking, dripping, and sniffles always followed me to sleep. Sage would figure it out. He was the smartest person I knew. I trusted him.

The memories faded. I didn't even know if they were real or something I'd imagined.

I was so cold. Curled into a ball, I warmed my hands between my thighs. My eyes traced the outline of the two doors in the room. I wasn't inside a cage. I could go to the door and try it, escape. I should. My brain kept telling me to do that, but everything else kept me on that smelly tattered mattress crying. The plumbing was still bad in the place and water dripped from somewhere. The only sound in the world.

Get up, Jordan. I heard Sage's disappointment in his voice. *Try the door. The least you could do.*

Try the door.

I rubbed my palms against my jeans and slowly

climbed to my feet. Dizzy at first, I waited until it passed. "I could do this," I whispered." I could. All I had to do was reach out my hand, touch the doorknob, and turn. That's it. Nothing more. The door would do the rest. Just turn it.

But moving closer felt as if I were pushing a wall of stone. I had to drag my feet across the dirty floor as if they weighed a ton. My heart rattled, sweat broke out making me cold.

It's just a door. A stupid door.

I couldn't remember which door led to the stairs. I chose the one on the right. Right is right, right? I almost giggled at my own madness. I lifted my hands. The weight crushed me. It hurt. Everything hurt. From my brain to the bottom of my feet hurt. A few inches. It's all I'd have to reach, just a few inches. My fingers were so close, I could feel the cool knob just under my fingertips when the door buckled. Something slammed into it on the other side. The knob rattled. I jolted back, falling hard on my ass. Pain zipped up my spinal column to my head. A scream blasted on the other side.

No, not a scream. A voice. One I recognized.

"Jordan! Jordan, oh, God, please. Are you there?"

Vicky.

I felt something snap inside of me. Instead of going to the door, I crawled away. I couldn't. "Vicky!" Tears burst out of me. "Vicky, you have to run. Please. No. Please. You have to run."

"I can't. There's nothing on this side." She tried the door again. Kicking it, panting, scratching.

I could do nothing but cover my ears and rock myself back and forth. "I'm sorry. I'm sorry."

"You should be." The voice behind me made me yelp and I crawled away from it. Away from Vicky and the door. Away from the man and his cold words and cold eyes. "Though it's not going to save you," Sloane said.

I stopped crawling when I didn't have anywhere else to go and hugged my knees. Sloane crouched down to my eye level. His eyes reached into my soul and yanked out something cold, something dark. "Bellamy Martinez." His voice sent chills up my spine. "Hmm, let me see." He ticked up one finger. "Sage died at the scene. Poor Rufus and Abigail Harris. Lost their only son Matthew. You know the Harrises, don't you, Jordan?" He tsked. "I wonder how kind they'd be to you if they knew you were responsible for their son's death."

I shook my head, opened my mouth to deny it, but then clamped it shut when he lifted a second finger.

"Then there was Caper, who died for writing that fucking book. Then Peppermint led me to Rosemary. And now, you, Bellamy Martinez. Or better yet. Basil." He paused taking me in as if figuring out how he wanted to hurt me. "See, Vicky came to me the other day and told me all about you. She was hoping I'd help. Unlike everyone else in this town, she sees something good in you. Something worth saving. But we all know she's wrong." He ran his hand down his face. "And Aimee—" His voice broke. A moment of emotion came and went. Then he got to his feet. "How does it work, exactly? I threaten someone you care about, and you help me kill someone. Is that it?"

I swallowed the lump in my throat.

"Is that it!" Spittle fell from his mouth. He breathed, composed himself. "I'm going to kill Vicky if you don't give me the information I need. So, tell me, *Bellamy*," he hissed. "Where is Kale?"

Kale. Liam. My brother. The one I'd been charged to protect. I shook my head. "I don't know."

"Lie!" he yelled. "You do know and she's going

to die because of it. Is that what you want? For her to die?"

I shook my head. "No. Please. I'm sorry."

The crack to my face was quick and hard. White spots danced behind my eyes, and I tasted blood.

"Stop saying that. Sorry won't bring her back." He waited a few seconds before he sighed. "Very well. When you bury her, know it's your fault."

He rushed to the door on the right, turned the knob with one hand, preparing for the onslaught that came when he threw the door open. Vicky launched herself at him, all fingernails and teeth, but he was stronger. I shut my eyes and could do nothing but hear her scream.

The Parents usually took days to stop the screams. Sloane either lacked the patience or didn't have time because it must've been a few minutes later when he charged out of the room. The now silent room. I kicked and flailed to get away from him, but it didn't matter. He was so much bigger than me. And angrier.

"We were victims too!" I screamed.

A boot crunched down on my knee. The sound that burst from my throat sounded inhuman. I curled myself into a ball but that didn't help. He kept kicking me until I thought I was going to pass out. I wished for it.

Then he pulled me up by my hair to my wobbly feet. "You're not going to die yet," he hissed in my face. He shoved me hard, and I fell hard. "I'll go easy if you give him up."

Liam.

I shook my head and blabbered something, but my mouth wouldn't work. I spat out blood instead. Nothing I said would help anyway. I knew that. I knew that because I remembered the screams behind the door. I remembered Sage's words. "If we don't do what they say, they'll kill them at the scene. But if we bring them here, they'll have a chance at survival. They don't always have to die." He'd been wrong. They always died.

Sloane lifted me up again, this time he held me in a chokehold, his hot breath behind me. "You are nothing but a byproduct of evil."

That had been what my mother believed. The reason she'd taken me away from the world. She thought the trauma would lead me to become a violent psychopath. Maybe she was right. Maybe. But I still felt guilty. "What about *her?*" I cried. "Vicky's innocent!"

"And she'll die like all the other innocents. Sometimes they die."

"Aimee's alive," I blurted.

For a fraction of a second, he stiffened. His arm slackened. His breathing deepened.

"She's alive. If you go back, maybe you can help her. Make sure she doesn't go to prison. You...you can take all the blame." Even as I said those words, I knew they were useless.

I was dead.

To prove me right, he shoved me to the door. The left one. My bruised body screamed at me. My left knee was useless and I leaned on my right leg as I scrambled up the steps with him right behind me, shoving me outside and into the cold. I slipped on ice and fell on the snow.

In only a thermal shirt and jeans, there was nothing to abate the cold. It didn't matter anyway. I'd be dead in a little while. My body temperature would drop during the process of decay. He grabbed me again and dragged me away from the house. I knew where he was taking me. I knew. I recognized the tree and the boy shaded by it.

Sage.

I blinked my eyes, and he was still there. With me. Sage had always been with me. In the grave, then the woods as I followed Nana clutching Teddy close to my chest. It'd taken me what felt like hours to find the adult to save us. I'd been too late to save him though.

He lingered near that tree, crouched like he used to be whenever we were given free time in the yard. It had been gated once. It wasn't now. It had been taken care of, the grass thick and green, manicured by the six of us. Now it grew weeds and wildflowers. The fenced-in yard had been torn down. The house itself sloped inward in decay, like the haunted it housed inside.

Sloane shoved me hard next to the graves. "This is where they ended up. Here! Look!" I turned to look at the road he was pointing to. "Two miles! Two fucking miles from town!"

I shook my head. "We didn't know! I'm sorry!"

He swung at me.

I didn't stop saying I'm sorry. Not even when he lifted me up on my knees and put the gun to my head. "I'm sorry. I'm sorry. I'm sorry."

"Close your eyes, Basil. And you won't see the monsters," Sage whispered inside my head.

I closed my eyes.

"Let *sorry* take you to your grave," he said.

Then the world exploded, and I fell over. Still breathing, I couldn't tell where I'd been shot. Maybe it would take time for my body to realize it was dead. I still breathed in shallow breaths. Then I heard the crunch of snow. A presence over me and a deep cry so loud I thought the earth shook.

"No!" Strong arms wrapped around me. "No, please God, I can't lose him again."

Again.

My eyes wouldn't open. I'm sure they were

swollen shut. Some parts of my body hurt, the other parts too cold to feel anything. I don't know what was better.

I felt hands on my face, brushing my hair away. "Mijo, open your eyes. Please, open your eyes." The voice thick with emotion. "I'm sorry," the man cried. "I'm sorry I wasn't there. I didn't protect you. I'm so sorry."

I felt myself being rocked in strong arms. Sirens rang in the distance. Something warm was wrapped around me, and I was lifted from the ground. I burrowed into the warm, strong chest, feeling the strong heartbeat against my body.

"Dad." The word slipped out of my mouth right before I passed out.

ELIZABETH ARROYO

Chapter Thirty-Seven

I'd been kidnapped three times in my life. Once when I was two and the Batemans took me from the park while my mother went to grab me an ice cream. Then when my biological mom took me to protect me from the bad people, or myself. She was afraid I'd become like the Batemans one day with all the trauma I'd experienced as a kid. And I'd been kidnapped when Sloane took me and tried to kill me. Special Agent Nate Martinez only found me because of Liam's ridiculous plan of using me as bait. He'd put a tracker in my shoe. The annoying pebble in my shoe had saved my life. I wanted to both punch him in the face and kiss him for that.

But my life hadn't been all bad. When Victoria Manning picked me to take home, she'd made my life better. She'd worked at the hospital as a nurse. She went to Sunday Mass like a good Christian. She always volunteered to do things for the town. She loved this town and the people loved her. Her hospital room was an explosion of flowers and chocolates. Well, just flowers now. I may have eaten the chocolates. The important thing was that Vicky had survived.

I'd woken up after a day to Special Agent Nate Martinez sleeping in the chair next to me. I took a quick inventory of my injuries. My ribs hurt. Broken, probably. My face was swollen like a melon. One eye closed, the other almost closed. My knee had to be set in a cast, and it itched like a mother. "You failed," I said grumpily to Special Agent Nate Martinez. Despite his closed eyes, I knew he was awake.

"With what?" he asked without opening his eyes.

"Protecting me," I said.

Then I had passed out.

After a few days, I'd been allowed to sit in Vicky's room. She'd been worse off than me. Sloane had stabbed her repeatedly and she had lost her right leg. She was still groggy most of the time. But she was alive.

Special Agent Martinez stayed with me in Vicky's room. He followed me everywhere. And when he didn't, SA Ferrell would. I wanted to blame Special Agent Martinez for everything. But I knew that was unfair. He had saved me this time. I knew the other times weren't his fault. They weren't anyone's fault but the Batemans. I just liked making him prickly. That's the word Vicky had used when I told her that Special Agent Nate Martinez was my dad. She knew, of course.

I got to my feet and the world shifted slightly. But Special Agent Nate Martinez was there, holding my elbow. I hadn't even heard him move. Without a word, he helped me untangle myself from the wires. Once that was done, he helped me into a robe, and then onto a wheelchair. My left leg extended in its cast. He pushed me into the elevator, and we took it to the third floor. During the whole process, he'd said nothing.

"You don't say much, do you."

"I'm afraid not."

He was frustrating.

Sheriff Jack Johnson was in the room with another bunch of flowers in his hand. When Vicky saw me, she smiled. Smiled! And my heart did all sorts of things. Her cheeks were rosy, her eyes vibrant.

Special Agent Martinez pushed me close to her bed.

"Mom," I said and took her offered hand and kissed her on the forehead.

After I told Special Agent Martinez that I didn't want to go with him, though he hadn't offered to take me anywhere, he told me that I still belonged to the state. That Vicky had never adopted me. Mrs. Lyle from the state even paid me a visit. I knew she would eventually have to take me back to the group home. I didn't want to go to the group home. But when I asked Vicky why she didn't adopt me, she said because she didn't have anything to really offer me. She was poor. I got the medicine and care from the state. I'd also be eligible for state scholarships for school if I was a ward. She couldn't afford those things because she sent money to her sister in Missoula for her mother's care. Her sister, Audrey, came to visit Vicky too. She was a hard-looking woman with pale blonde hair, dark blue eyes, and frown lines etched on her face. But there were a few moments I caught her holding Vicky's hand when Vicky slept. And tears. Maybe some families can't show their emotions so readily. Maybe that too had something to do with memories.

"You look better than all these flowers in the room," I boasted, trying to put cheer in my voice. That was hard considering I didn't do cheer and my face still hurt.

But her smile was so worth it.

"Thank you, my handsome son," she said.

Since she woke up, I took to calling her mom and she took to calling me son. It made her smile. Win. Win.

Her eyes lifted to Special Agent Nate Martinez. He bowed slightly and said, "Vicky." As if he wanted her to know he knew her name.

"Special Agent Nate Martinez is a man of little words," I said, going for a whisper but not really making it.

Vicky squeezed my hand. She did that when she thought I needed some strength. "The pot calling the kettle black," she said.

I scowled. "Huh?"

She laughed. That she could laugh without grimacing sent joy through me. Jack started to laugh too. It was nice. He was nice to hear, at least. And she deserved nice. Special Agent Martinez chuckled. Just chuckled, looking at me with a glint to his eye as if still wondering if I was Bellamy, his dead son.

I still wasn't sure, honestly.

While I was still at the hospital, Special Agent Nate Martinez pushed an emergency order with the State of Montana to remove me from foster care. He corrected my death record and Jordan Brooks died a silent death, replaced by Bellamy Jordan Martinez. Special Agent Martinez added the Jordan name for me. Mrs. Cooper had suggested keeping things stable for my sanity. I agreed with her.

While Vicky was at the hospital and he was finishing up the case in the FBI office in Missoula, I stayed with Liam and his family.

I know it was weird, but I missed Aimee sometimes. They charged her as an adult, and she'd be going to state prison when she turns eighteen. I still saw her face in my nightmares. I woke up screaming sometimes. Liam held me those nights and I held him when he screamed too. Mrs. Grant finally added an adjacent room to Liam's with a shared curtain we could use to get to each other at night. Sometimes I slept on his bed, or he'd sleep on mine. Dr. Cooper said we had to be careful not to grow dependent on each other again. She gave us parameters, but we didn't follow them. We'd figure it out as we go. That's what Liam said, and I agreed.

Memories are an odd thing. They pulsed like blood flowing through arteries. Some memories were distortions of sights, scents, sounds, and feelings. All interpreted by a confused mind. Where I remembered safety in the embrace of my cage mate, Liam remembered cold and dark fears. Where I remembered the paralyzing fear that made me cry, Liam remembered the strength I'd shown. He'd even called me brave. Even if I was still afraid of doors.

Dr. Cooper said that we'd work around my past now that we both knew who I really was, and the reason behind my fears, but that my full memories might never return. When the Batemans abducted me, the long-term memory database in my brain hadn't been fully developed. It didn't make me abnormal. It made me lucky. That's what Liam said anyway. He remembered everything.

Liam, Chase, and I visited the Harrises. Mrs. Harris gave me a picture of Matthew. The one she had on her mantel. He wore a soccer shirt. His eyes were wide and happy. He'd been six in the picture. The last time they saw him. I remembered bits and pieces of his face, but his eyes had never changed. I don't know why I didn't piece it together before.

"Matthew Harris," I started, running my fingers along his picture. "Your son had snuck me out while he'd been digging the grave of Elise Cooper."

Chase squeezed my thigh and tears pooled at the edge of his eyes. He blinked and they fell.

"I was the youngest of the group so the Batemans wouldn't miss me as fast as they would anyone else. Sometimes, they'd let me roam the house and play with Nana, our dog. Matthew came up with a brilliant plan to save them." I lifted my eyes to the Harrises. They were holding each other, watching me. Tears gleamed in their eyes. Even Mr. Harris, who was strong and brave. "That's what he said, them, not us. *Them.* As if he knew what it would cost to save us."

Mrs. Harris sobbed silently into Mr. Harris's shoulder. The guy was so big. She looked so small.

"Eventually, I found an adult. Gave them the message Matthew had given me to give to them, and we were saved."

Liam got to his feet, his eyes bloodshot. Tears falling down his face. Mr. and Mrs. Harris looked up at him. They didn't startle him. He looked ready to run, hands clenched, eyes seeing but unseeing. He swallowed a few times, then in a small whisper he said, "I'm sorry," and walked out.

"My boy was brave," Mr. Harris said.

I nodded. "Yes. Yes, he was very brave. He…" I looked down at the picture. "He was a hero." I swallowed the lump in my own throat. "The town council is tearing down the Batemans' farm and erecting a memorial. I'd like to add something special for Matthew, if that'd be okay."

Mrs. Harris took my hands. Her smile was sad but bright too. "We'd like that, Jordan. Very much."

When we walked out of the house, Liam was standing next to Chase's truck and we hugged. He sobbed into my shoulder. Chase didn't say anything. He let us have our moment. Then Liam let me go and climbed into the truck and Chase turned me around and kissed me. The kiss was soft and I knew he tasted my tears too. Then he hugged me.

People came from everywhere to the inauguration of the memorial. A stone had been erected with the names of the victims. A statue of a young boy stood on top of the rock. The carving had managed to catch Matthew's beautiful eyes. Matthew no longer haunted me, and I missed him so much.

I met all of the Harrises that day. I mean ALL of them. They came from the southern lands, Florida,

California, everywhere. And they were all as kind as Mr. and Mrs. Harris. The town had a festival with a lot of food, drinks, and dancing.

I met Dakota's mom that day. She had donated all of the proceeds from Dakota's book to help missing and exploited children. It had been what Dakota had wanted all along. To help the lost ones. Just like us.

Sheriff Johnson proposed to Vicky the day she got out of the hospital. I was there with her, which felt weird. So was Finn. Who kept his distance. But Sheriff Johnson had gotten down on one knee, opened a box, and proposed.

For a fraction, I saw the happiness in her face. The love. Like when she looked at me. But she cupped his hand and lowered the box. "Jack, I don't come alone." Then she looked at me.

Everything with Special Agent Nate Martinez being my dad was still up in the air, but she still chose me. I wanted to cry. Okay, maybe I did cry.

"We…" Sheriff Johnson looked at Finn who looked like he wanted to be absorbed by the wall at his back. "We made changes to the house. I'd like you to see. Both of you."

And we did.

Sheriff Johnson had given me Finn's old bedroom and put Finn in the guest room. My room had its own bathroom with a thick curtain. And the bedroom door had a sliding door fitted inside. No knobs. No locks. That he loved her enough to do this for her melted her heart and she said yes. And they were engaged.

Special Agent Nate Martinez and Vicky explained that I'd be living with both her and him as if they were a divorced couple sharing custody. Except I knew Vicky didn't have any legal rights to make decisions or anything, Special Agent Nate Martinez would allow it on certain conditions.

I had to stop being an ass with him.

Well, he didn't say it like that. But that's the interpretation I got from it.

Special Agent Nate Martinez bought a house near Liam's property he called a fixer upper. He said that he wanted to experience the Montana mountains with his family, and I'd have my own room with my own bathroom and a push plate door. He planned on moving in with his family at the end of the school year in two months. He wanted his son Nate Jr. to finish eighth grade in New York before relocating. It meant Nate Jr. and I would be attending White Falls High School together next year.

I met his family during Christmas break. It was weird. Sadie, seven, liked to wear a tutu and dance everywhere, even though she wasn't really good at it. Mrs. Martinez said she'd learn or grow out of it but that I should probably not tell her how awful she dances so I smiled and lied. Nate Jr. didn't talk to me at all. He was upset about the move to White Falls. He'd be leaving his friends behind and everything he'd ever known. At one point, when he asked me why I acted like a nutjob, I thought Special Agent Martinez was going to fold and make me stay in New York. I told him I didn't mind living with Vicky full time until I graduated high school, and then I'd be going to college, but he said no and sent Nate Jr. to his room. I was glad when I finally came back home.

Riley and I were accepted into Chase's group of bandmates and jocks. Riley even made the lacrosse team and played horribly. But he did get very animated cheers from team Liam. I think Liam has a crush on him.

Chase and I came out to everyone. He decided that my proclamation of love—even under duress—

warranted an official status of boyfriend. So, Chase and I held hands at school, and we even found kissing spots behind things, like trees, buildings, and the bleachers.

Jaylene still hated me, but she no longer hurt Chase. The book had affected her, and Mrs. Cooper finally admitted her into the mental wellness ward at the hospital. Chase had a very serious talk with his family about what he expected to happen when she got out. He wasn't going to be her punching bag anymore. They had a very special moment with tears and all. Jaylene's at baseline now. Which was good.

After a few months, I finally felt normal. Whatever that meant.

"Hey."

I looked up from my art book to Chase plopping down beside me on the sofa. It sank with his weight, and I leaned into him, taking a whiff of his sweaty scent. Peppermint, no weed. He wiped the sweat off his face with the hem of his t-shirt. He'd finished practice with Monkey Swine. The rest of the guys took their places in front of the TV in the living room in Liam's guesthouse where they practiced every day. They had a big gig coming up. Liam snatched the game system control from Riley who was on the verge of rage quitting. "You suck, dude," Liam said with a smirk and proceeded to outplay Riley, who snatched glances at him with a look.

The look.

I quirked a smile.

"What're you smiling about?"

"Nothing." I wasn't about to out my best friend.

Chase kissed my smile away. He did that a lot. Mostly, when I was looking at Liam. Chase would swoop in and kiss me. I loved his kisses. I kinda loved him too, I think. I was still trying to figure out the names of all my emotions.

"So," I began as he peppered kisses along my jaw. "Why Monkey Swine?"

The kisses reached my earlobe. "Why not?" he whispered against the shell of my ear, sparking a line of heat down my neck, arm, and lower.

"Well, that's not normal. It's actually a genetically engineered chimera."

He chuckled as his lips grazed my jaw. "You looked it up."

Heat rushed up to my cheeks. "Yeah. Maybe."

He shrugged and dug his nose into the crook of my neck, then sucked my earlobe again. "Who wants to be normal anyway? Normal's boring. I don't want normal."

My heart did a little jump. "I'm not normal," I said as his lips touched mine.

"Exactly."

Chase kissed me and I tossed normal out the window. Metaphorically.

I'd been surrounded by death my whole life.

Death led me to the Harrises.

Death led me to my biological father.

Death led me back to the place I'd forgotten to face the door.

Death led me to Chase Cooper and for the first time, I looked forward to what life held for me. I hoped it was more kisses.

The End

Evernight Teen

www.evernightteen.com